PSI SUCCESSFUL BU

Developing Company Policies

Ready-To-Use Models For Small Business

By Ardella Ramey and Carl R. J. Sniffen

The Oasis Press® / PSI Research
Grants Pass, Oregon

Published by The Oasis Press

Developing Company Policies

This publication is designed to provide accurate and authoritative information in regard to the subject matter covered. It is sold with the understanding that the publisher is not engaged in rendering legal, accounting, or other professional service. If legal advice or other expert assistance is required, the services of a competent professional person should be sought.

—from a declaration of principles jointly adopted by a committee of the American Bar Association and a committee of publishers

Page and Forms Formatting: Melody Joachims
Editorial Assistance: Vickie Reierson

Please direct any comments, questions, or suggestions regarding this book to The Oasis Press, Editorial Department, at the address below.

The Oasis Press offers PSI Successful Business Software for sale. For information, contact:

PSI Research
300 North Valley Drive
Grants Pass, OR 97526
(503) 479-9464

The Oasis Press is a Registered Trademark of Publishing Services, Inc., a Texas corporation doing business in Oregon as PSI Research.

ISBN 1-55571-125-1

Printed in the United States of America
First edition 10 9 8 7 6 5 4 3 2 1 Revision Code: AAA

Printed on recycled paper when available.

Table of Contents

Charts, Forms, and Outlines

Foreword

Sound human resource policy is a necessity in the growth of any business or company. Recognition of this necessity may occur when management realizes that an increasing amount of time is being devoted to human resource issues: time that could be devoted to production, marketing, and planning for growth. Effective, consistent, and fair human resource decisions are often made more time consuming by a lack of written, standardized policies and procedures. Moreover, when issues concerning employee rights and company policies come before federal and state courts, the decisions generally regard company policies, whether written or verbal, as being a part of an employment contract between the employee and the company. Without clearly written policies, the company is at a disadvantage.

Developing Company Policies has been created for small to mid-size businesses generally employing fewer than 20 employees. It is designed to help your business develop clearly-written policies by providing a source of model personnel policies.

Developing Company Policies contains those basic policies the authors feel most employers should include in a policy manual. Of course,not all of the policies contained in this book may be required by your business.

You may also require additional policies which are not addressed in this book. In this situation, please consult the comprehensive manual *A Company Policy and Personnel Workbook* published by The Oasis Press. More than 50 additional policies can be found there including policies covering sexual harassment, substance abuse, employee safety, educational assistance, child care, conflicts of interest, grievance procedures, recreational activities, employee security and employer privacy. Companion software is also available for *A Company Policy and Personnel Workbook.*

The authors' acknowledgment is given to the many persons who so generously gave of their time in providing suggestions to the development of this book, in particular, the employees at PSI Research in Grants Pass, Oregon.

Introduction

This book was written to help you make efficient use of your time in developing a cohesive and up-to-date policy manual. The person or committee who is assigned the responsibility of writing the manual will find that this book makes the whole process of selecting, understanding, and tailoring personnel policies much easier than having to research and construct them from scratch.

Before beginning this process, consider some of the benefits that your company can gain from a policy manual:

- A set of written guidelines for human resource decisions;
- A means of communication with employees;
- A framework for consistency and fairness;
- A way to promote the company philosophy;
- A tool for saving management time; and
- A means of protecting the legal interests of the company.

Consider each of these benefits in more detail.

1. A set of written guidelines for human resource decisions — The process that you will undertake in comparing the policy alternatives, understanding their importance, and evaluating your current practices will help you develop your company's guidelines and procedures.
2. A means of communication with employees — The policy manual serves first and foremost as a way to communicate with employees. It demonstrates awareness of and interest in employees' individual security needs. It helps to organize and announce management's plans for growth, and it communicates the company's investment in its employees.
3. A framework for consistency and fairness — The policy manual defines management's standards for making decisions on various personnel and organizational issues. The clearly defined procedures and standards express the company's intent to make consistent and evenhanded decisions.
4. A way to promote the company philosophy — The policies will reflect the company's philosophy of business and employee relations as they demonstrate:
    - Your creativity in solving policy issues;
    - The competitive position of the company in providing a variety of employee benefits; and
    - The respect and appreciation for human resource management.

5. A tool for saving management time — Carefully drafted and standardized policies and procedures save the company countless hours of management time. The consistent use and interpretation of such policies, in an evenhanded and fair manner, reduces management's concern about legal issues becoming legal problems.
6. A means of protecting the legal interests of a company — A company's policies and procedures define the rights and obligations of the employee and of the company. In that sense, the policy manual is an expression of the rules governing the employment relationship. In the 1990s, probably more so than ever before, a company must protect its rights within that relationship by adopting policies that are fair to both sides, clearly stated and legally permissible.

The discussion of the above six points will help clarify the responsibility that you accept in developing your policy manual. The authors own experiences and research have helped provide the information throughout this book, and the next three sections in this introduction will outline a process to help you easily develop your policy manual.

Throughout this book, you will see the terms "you" and "management." It is the authors' intent that the term "you" refers to the business owner. The term "management" refers to those other company officers or employees who assist the owner in managing the business. In many small businesses, the owner of the business performs all or substantially all management functions, and if this description fits your business, the terms "you" and "management" are synonymous.

Develop and Maintain Your Policy Manual

Developing Company Policies is designed to assist your business by providing clearly-written policies that balance employee and employer rights and expectations as well as take the drudgery out of developing policies from scratch.

As a business owner, you must be directly involved in the development of the manual and its presentation to employees. A committee should be selected from employees, the size of which will vary depending on the size of the company and management's willingness to broaden the process. Broader representation will bring different viewpoints and perspectives to the discussions and help to develop a better set of policies. The involvement of management ensures that the company philosophies regarding business, production, and employee satisfaction, among others, will be found within the manual.

Here are some suggestions the committee can follow when developing the policy manual.

- Select a person on the committee to coordinate development of the manual;
- Study this book to become familiar with its contents and the **Comment** sections;
- Meet with management to delineate what is to be accomplished by the manual;
- Determine which present company policies will be included in the manual and whether or not they need to be revised;
- Have supervisors/managers respond to a checklist of tentative policies and an outline of instructions for implementing policies; and
- Set deadlines and arrange for progress reports.

Another important responsibility of the committee is a training session to introduce the policy and personnel manual to all employees. If this is your first manual, consider an employee–orientation meeting during which:

- The company president comments on the importance of the manual and its purposes;
- One or more of the committee members involved in developing the manual presents a brief discussion of its organization, each of its policies, and the reasons for including them in the manual; and
- Time for questions and comments from the employees.

If your company has made only revisions to current, established policies, or is adding only a few new policies, a more informal meeting would be appropriate. An important part of the process, prior to introducing the manual to your employees, is to have the company attorney review its contents.

The manual's publication does not complete the project. As the company grows and the workforce becomes larger and more diverse, new issues will have to be faced and new policies developed to cover them. Similarly, changes in laws, regulations, employee benefits, and other areas will necessitate revisions. You may choose to maintain the committee to make revisions or for new policy development. Or you may appoint one person, possibly a committee member or department head, for this purpose. Whoever is responsible should have access to the committee's notes, research, drafts of discarded policies, and meeting minutes for reference. A master file should be created and indexed by policy number to store the materials, including management memos regarding policy issues. A record of revisions should be maintained when changes to a policy are made. These records can save valuable time when drafting revisions or looking for policy alternatives.

When the policy manual is published, consider numbering each copy and having a master log which identifies the person or department that received each manual. Numbering the manuals assists in their distribution and revision as well as maintaining control of them. Employees should also sign a statement indicating their receipt of the policy manual. You may not want the manual distributed outside of the company or kept by employees who leave the company.

Lastly, you may want the committee or a committee member to be the sole source of policy and procedure interpretation. Whoever has this responsibility must have access to the developmental records and be aware of the changes in management's desires and philosophies. To ensure evenhanded and fair treatment of employees, an important interpretation of a policy should be documented, including the facts giving rise to the issue. These interpretations are valuable as precedents for future use.

Suggested Formats for Your Policy Manual

There are several formats available to you when organizing your policy manual. This section discusses loose-leaf, numeric, and alphabetical organizational formats as well as assists you in determining your manual's size, binding, and printing options. To help accomplish this, answer these questions:

- What is the image your company wants to portray to employees through the policy and procedures manual?
- How much money is budgeted for the manual?
- What method of upkeep of the manual will the company initiate—that is, will employee manuals be returned to one location for updating, or will updated policies be distributed and employees expected to maintain their own manuals?
- Does the assigned work location of employees have an effect on the type of manual that should be selected? For example, are they working at a desk or are they assigned to trucks out in the field?
- Do you anticipate major revisions in the manual in the next couple of years?

Here are some general points to consider regarding the content of policies.

- Keep in mind who the policies are written for.
- Organize each policy in a logical operational sequence.
- Stay on the subject.
- Make sentences and paragraphs short.
- Avoid rigid formality.
- Check for understanding; be flexible but avoid vague, unclear, or indirect statements.

If you choose the loose-leaf binder format for your manual, we suggest that your company name or logo be prominent on each page. The section name and policy title on each page help in organizing and referencing the manual. The use of "page ___ of ___ pages" makes it easy for everyone to determine if he or she has the complete policy in their manual. The use of "effective date" and "revision date" assists in researching the history and changes to each policy. The inclusion of "Approved by" legitimizes the policy and ensures that policy language has been reviewed by the responsible person. We have provided a sample policy format at the end of this introduction which incorporates these aids.

Your company will probably already have an established terminology for key words that should be used throughout the manual, such as references to gender, organization, department, division, and positions. You may easily alter the policies in this book to continue this terminology or, in some cases, you may wish to make changes to clarify your in-house communication.

The authors have chosen to use his or her when referring to employees; however, there are some other choices you can consider using.

- Instead of his or her, you could use the word, "the". For example, you could say, "return to the shift" rather than "return to his or her shift."
- Write a disclaimer statement in the introduction of the manual stating the use of either a masculine or feminine gender which will refer to both his and her alike; or
- You could simply use the word, "person".

Throughout this book, the vice president is referred to in a number of the policies as the company's chief administrator of the policies set forth in the manual. You may choose to alter this reference to more adequately serve your company's needs. The role and responsibilities taken by your company's vice president, if any, will determine your need to tailor each policy. (For more information, refer to the following section, How to Use this Book.) As you select the appropriate department or individual title reference, consider the role and responsibilities of the respective department or person as well as the image management wishes to communicate to employees. In some cases, especially in small companies, one person, such as a vice president, is responsible for all personnel duties and operations. Because what you do in implementing the policy can be as important as what is said in the manual, careful attention must be given to ensure that personnel administrators and supervisors/managers have the skills to understand the manual's contents and to deal with company employees in a responsive and caring manner.

In selecting a person or persons to administer or implement the manual, keep two things in mind. First, the manual should clearly identify who is responsible for administering and implementing the manual. With this information, employees will know where to direct their comments and questions about various policies. Second, the persons charged with the responsibility of administering or implementing the policies must understand their duties and have a good working knowledge of the policy manual's contents.

Numeric and alphabetic formats are commonly used when organizing personnel and policy manuals. If you select the numeric format, incorporate a flexible numbering system so that your company can add more statements without having to renumber the system each time; for example, 600.1–Welcome Letter from the President, 600.2–Equal Opportunity, 600.3–Equal Pay; or 100–Welcome Letter from the President, 200–Equal Opportunity, 300–Equal Pay. The policies under these headings would then be assigned in tens, ones, or additional decimals. For example, regarding 600.1–Welcome Letter from the President, you would number any subsections and their respective policies in the following manner: Company History–600.1.1 or 110, Continuity of Policies–600.1.2 or 120; thus, allowing for other policies relating to Company History to be assigned 600.1.1.1 or 111, 112. In selecting an alphabetical format, the same considerations should be followed. Usually a combination of alphabetic and numeric is chosen, e.g., A-1-b.

Some companies have a less-detailed, informational employee handbook which dwells less on company procedures than a policy and procedures manual would. In this case, the policy manual is usually distributed to management or supervisory personnel only, whereas all employees are given the employee handbook. For convenience and clarity, it is also wise to select the same organizational format if you plan to issue an employee handbook.

To reduce the cost of reprinting a bound booklet, it is advisable to adopt the loose-leaf format; however, circumstances may not make this format practical in all cases, such as when the policies must be used "in the field" where a large notebook would be cumbersome. If this is the case, the authors recommend that only one policy be placed on any individual page or pages. We also recommend that 10% of the pages be left blank. If any policy needs to be revised, or if policies are to be added, the revision, or additional policies, can be printed on separate gummed sheets and glued over old policies or onto the blank pages. This practice can save printing or duplication cost until the revisions or additions become extensive enough to warrant printing a new bound version.

How to Use this Book

This book is organized into four chapters with each chapter featuring its own introduction and selection of alternate policies. Chapter topics range from hiring practices to employee benefits and expenses. Each policy within the chapters has its own **Comment** section which is provided to give the staff and policy committee an overview of the considerations that should be discussed prior to developing that particular policy. If there are important federal laws relating to a policy, they are discussed within its **Comment** section. These **Comment** portions of the book sometimes refer to California statutes and case law regarding the policy issues; however, these citations are inserted for emphasis only and to alert you that other states may have the same or similar rules. The remaining 49 states have not necessarily followed California's rules; but in many instances, California has been a leading state in adopting modern rules regarding employment law. Regardless, this book was written for use by companies located throughout the United States and not solely for California employers.

Throughout this book, the authors use **Note** and italicize subsequent warnings or reminders for you to research for any peculiarities or variations in your state's laws or to take action on other important related issues. (Be sure your typist deletes any **Notes** when typing policy drafts or final copies.) It is always advisable to consult your company attorney or legal counsel before your policy manual is printed and distributed throughout the company because of the variations in state laws.

The policies in this book are integrated to be used as a complete policy manual with a minimum amount of tailoring; however, some companies may choose to expand upon some policies when special circumstances warrant. If you would like to make changes to a policy, its **Comment** section will help you tailor the wording.

For easier and more effective use of this book, the authors suggest you freely use pencils and various-colored highlight pens to make this a working document. As you read the following chapters, make use of the margins or space at the bottom of a page to jot down your ideas or to make notes of the issues you want to clarify or discuss with management. Use colored highlight pens to identify specifics you want covered in policies (e.g., yellow); federal or state laws you want to discuss with your company attorney for further clarification (e.g., red); and alternatives that you want to explore with other committee members (e.g., green). This book is planned to be your organizer as well as a working document.

You may have noticed the three-digit numbers in the Table of Contents as well as in the following chapters after each policy title. The purpose of these three-digit numbers is to provide an easy-to-follow, chronological numbering system for this book's policy sections and their respective alternate policies.

The first digit of the section number indicates which chapter the policy is located in, and the subsequent two numbers indicate its chronological listing within that particular chapter. For example, in the text, the authors may refer you to Section 200 on Equal Opportunity. By using the section number, you would know the section is located in Chapter 2 and would be listed chronologically by using the last two numbers. The three-digit number is also used as a prefix in the number which identifies and lists any alternate policies contained within a policy section. So, any alternate policies listed in Section 200, would have the following identification numbers: 200.1, 200.2, and 200.3, etc.

Many of the policies have alternate statements for your comparison and selection. The authors give no preference or priority to the Alternate Policy 1 versus the Alternate Policy 2. Write your policies as they will be implemented within your company, considering the policies as means to an end, not ends in themselves.

Select the policies to be included in your manual by asking these questions.

- Are we required by federal or state law or contract to have this policy?
- What is the reason for having this policy?
- Does our organization with its size, business, and work force justify having this policy?
- Does enforcing this policy accomplish our company goals?
- Is the policy consistent with the company's management or business philosophy?
- What have we done in the past to solve issues related to this policy?
- Does this policy strike a proper balance between management flexibility and fairness to employees?
- Is the cost, such as the time and expense, of administering this policy reasonable in relationship to the benefits to be obtained?

As you select policies to be included in your manual, refer back to these questions to make certain that your policy will strike a balance between fairness to your employees and flexibility and cost effectiveness for your business.

Select the policies that you want to include in your manual and place the other policies in the back of this book for future reference or consideration. Select only those policies you need and which you are willing to devote adequate time, expense, and resources.

Read the **Comment** section, highlighting the points which you believe your committee should discuss together or with management prior to developing your company's policy statement.

Read Alternate Policy 1 to see if it covers your company's main objectives and management's philosophies. Then read Alternate Policy 2 and ask yourself:

- How does each policy relate to the points highlighted in the **Comment** section?
- Is this the solution to our problem?
- Is this a procedure we can implement?

For your convenience, the alternate policies have been double spaced for making changes to the statements or adding statements unique to your company. You may pick and choose parts of each of the two alternate policies and combine them into one. Avoid contradictions within one policy and ensure that other related policies are consistent with that policy.

Throughout the policies in this book, the job title of the individual whom your employees should contact for additional information, approval, or assistance is indicated by (VICE PRESIDENT). You should use or modify this title to fit your particular company's in-house communications and organization. Even though an individual's name may seem a wise choice, the policy may become outdated with the frequency of company promotions and employee mobility. Whenever (COMPANY) is used, you should replace it with your company's name. When your manual is complete, carefully proofread it to make certain that it is internally consistent, that is, that the appropriate departments or individuals are named or referred to throughout the manual.

If neither of the alternate policies reflects management's or employees' desires, use the **Comment** section and the alternate policies as a guide in developing your own policy. Keep in mind that the policies should comply with federal and state laws and regulations.

The authors strongly encourage the management team to monitor the types of human resource questions and concerns that confront the company, every few months, to determine when additional policies should be added or existing policies revised or deleted. Avoid writing a policy for every problem. It is important to weigh the burden of not having the policy against adding an unlimited number of policies. Allow a potential policy to simmer for 30 days before adding it to your manual. Also, consider a periodic group orientation to explain your policy manual to new employees and to answer any questions concerning it.

The policy manual is ready to be typed and reproduced once you have selected the policies, made changes, and tailored each policy. Select the format for the manual by reviewing the section, Suggested Formats for Your Manual, earlier in this introduction. Don't forget to ask the company attorney to review your manual for completeness and compliance with state and federal laws.

We suggest you start with a limited number of policies and add others as they become appropriate. Every three to six months, the individual or committee responsible for the manual should review its contents to determine if there should be any revisions or additions. A policy can also be deleted as the company outgrows the need for it. Keeping the manual current is also important: it communicates the importance of its contents to the employees, and it assists managers in their supervisory role. Such changes also signify to the employees that the company keeps up with the times and the competition. Remember, undefined policies and inconsistencies in policies consume a great amount of management time and become a hidden cost to the company, not to mention, unnecessary confusion and miscommunication among employees.

If you require additional policies which do not appear in this book, a comprehensive manual, *A Company Policy and Personnel Workbook* is available from The Oasis Press. It includes more than 50 additional policies, forms and outlines. Companion software for *A Company Policy and Personnel Workbook* is also available. Order forms for this valuable business tool are found at the end of this book.

Final Thoughts Before You Begin

Before you begin, some final thoughts merit consideration:

- What an employer does in practice is as important as what is written in the policy manual. The actions and words of management must be consistent with the manual.
- Don't include policies you don't understand and therefore cannot consistently or properly administer.
- Select persons charged with the responsibility of administering the policy manual with great care and skill. If managers and supervisors are not capable of uniformly and consistently applying the policies or if they lack good interpersonal skills, the policy manual will fail in its essential purposes.
- Recognize the nonstatic nature of business and the business environment, and be flexible and able to adapt to changes. Case law, statutes, and regulations change. Your policy manual must be able to change as well.
- Your manual should overstate the employer's rights to modify or terminate policies set forth in the manual at any time and from time to time. The manual must indicate that it is not to be considered a contract of employment.
- Treat employees within the same classification equally.
- Use good common sense.

A sample policy manual cover page follows and is provided for your convenience.

SAMPLE POLICY

PSI Research

Policy and Procedures Manual

EQUAL OPPORTUNITY POLICY — Policy Number 200.1

Equal Opportunity is PSI Research policy. It is PSI Research policy to select the best qualified person for each position in the organization. No employee of PSI Research will discriminate against an applicant for employment or fellow employee because of race, creed, color, religion, sex, national origin, ancestry, age, handicap or any other statutorily prohibited basis.

This policy applies to all employment practices and personnel actions. PSI Research has adopted an Affirmative Action policy which essentially means that the company will aggressively seek out, hire, develop and promote qualified members of protected groups (defined as racial minorities, women, physically or mentally handicapped, disabled veterans, veterans of the Vietnam era and persons between the ages of 40 to 70).

Any person having inquiries concerning PSI Research's compliance with the above is directed to contact the Vice President, who has been designated as Compliance Coordinator. The office is located at 300 North Valley Drive, Grants Pass, Oregon 97526; telephone (503) 479-9464.

Effective Date: 1/1/91

Revised: — Approved by: ____________________ President

Page 1 of __ pages

SAMPLE POLICY MANUAL COVER PAGE

[Company Name]

Policy Manual

The policies and procedures in this manual are not intended to be contractual commitments by (COMPANY), and they shall not be construed as such by employees. The policies and procedures are intended to be guides to management and are merely descriptive of suggested procedures to be followed. (COMPANY) reserves the right to revoke, change or supplement guidelines at any time without notice. No policy is intended as a guarantee of continuity of benefits or rights. No permanent employment or employment for any term is intended or can be implied from any statements in this manual.

[Company Name]
[Address]
[Date]

Chapter 1
Our Company

Introduction

The first section of your policy and personnel manual should describe your company. This will provide a brief overview of your company and welcome the new employee. Including this section in your manual is advantageous for several other reasons as well. The employees will learn something about the history of the company, who the founders are or were, and how the company got to where it is today. As an employee reads on, he or she will become aware of the company's objectives for growth and that he or she is a valuable participant in meeting those objectives. Although the policy manual is primarily designed to reveal how management will treat its employees and vice versa, you should also emphasize that it is designed to ensure that all employees know the company's organizational rules in order to succeed both individually and as a company. This section will give the employee a sense of what the company is all about and what he or she is a part of.

The amount and detail of information provided in this section will be determined, in part, by the number of employees and the age of the company. If the company is small and young, less information may be necessary. New employees joining the staff will probably interact with everyone and will quickly gain a perspective of the company. At some point in the company's growth, however, you will want to start developing the historical information for later use. And, regardless of how young your company is, an awareness of its history and its projected future is valuable to all employees.

The authors believe that you should have maximum flexibility in drafting the company policies. You or your management team already have adopted a way of communicating with your employees. Do not impose a structure which would be contrary to your company's current philosophy and style. Every company is unique and this section, more than others, is where that individuality really appears. Therefore, in this chapter, we have chosen to give you advice and suggestions on how to organize your policy manual's introduction rather than construct a policy or use language that might be uncomfortable for you. Because this initial section of your policy manual may take more thought, you may want to save it for last or work on it concurrently with other chapters.

Welcome Letter from the President 100

Comment: The president's letter welcomes new employees to the company. It is the first opportunity to set the tone of the manual and introduce the company philosophy. The letter may be a short welcome only, or it may include three or four sentences summarizing the history of the company, the number of company employees, the locations of other company offices, and the unique features about your company's product, service, and management. It may thank the employee for selecting the company as his or her place to work and stress the importance of becoming a productive part of the organization. But above all, the letter is a personal statement from the chief executive who is not only ultimately responsible for the company's fortunes but the policy manual as well.

Company History and Philosophy 110

Comment: A brief company history gives an employee a realization of the change and growth experienced by the company since its inception. Information about the founders of the company and a brief statement of their original objectives helps a new employee to gain an historical perspective and appreciate what the company has accomplished. Bear in mind that you want your employees to be just as proud of the company as you are, so do not be afraid to show them your pride. A few brief statements concerning the company's plans for the next two to five years depicts the leadership role of management in planning and preparing for the future. Planning may give employees a more secure feeling about the strength of the company.

Finally, it is generally accepted that employees are much happier and better workers when they respect the management of their company and believe their supervisors are competent, fair, and alert to employees' contributions. This statement of commitment can facilitate these beliefs. Some examples of general statements about the company's commitment to its employees include the following:

- The company's recruitment and selection of highly-capable and innovative employees;
- Management's commitment to provide a work environment and leadership which unites employees and generates enthusiasm for the company and its products and services;
- A commitment to maintain the highest standards of business ethics;
- An understanding of the importance of the employees' role in the company's success;
- A commitment to provide training and opportunities for advancement.

Depending on your management style, another commitment worth considering is an open-door policy. Specifically, the president or owner commits to being available to any employee at any convenient time to discuss any job-related problems that the employee may have. This is and especially valuable management technique for a small business. No manager likes to have an employee go over his or her head, but the effect that this commitment has on the responsiveness of supervisory personnel or middle management may be worthwhile to everyone.

Obviously, you must also commit to being fair and objective. If you manage this commitment well, the word will get out that you are responsive to every employee's problems. Your commitment to your employees is a statement of how you value them as people and how you intend to treat them. Your attitude toward management–employee relations will set the tone and style of employee–employer communications. These communications, and how you perform your commitments, have a significant impact on the work environment.

This subsection, or the welcoming letter, is the place to state your business and employee relations philosophy. You may not be able to state it as a commitment, but if you have a set of principles or rules for running your business, let your employees know what they are. Your wish to share the principles or philosophy with others reflects a leadership quality which will enhance respect for management and improve the work environment as much as anything else.

We have provided a sample Employee Orientation Checklist to guide management in providing individual or group orientation for introduction of the policy manual to employees.

EMPLOYEE ORIENTATION CHECKLIST

As a new employee, we would like to acquaint you with our policies and benefit programs so that your employment with us will be more rewarding. All employees, upon joining the staff at (COMPANY) will be asked to participate in an orientation. The orientation will be conducted by the (VICE PRESIDENT)

The following checklist will guide management in conducting and completing all phases of the orientation.

A. Issuing of Company Property

- ☐ Company Policy Manual
- ☐ Equipment Manuals
- ☐ Building Keys
- ☐ Alarm ID Card
- ☐ Other ______________________

B. Review of Company/Life at (COMPANY)

- ☐ Use of time clock/confirmation work hours
- ☐ Payday/Overtime
- ☐ Kitchen Use & Clean-up
- ☐ Meal and Rest Period/Smoking Policy
- ☐ No food in office area or work station
- ☐ Call management when late or absent
- ☐ Use of Telephone
- ☐ Parking
- ☐ Introductions
- ☐ Workman's Compensation

C. Company Policy (2nd week)

- ☐ Performance Review/Probation
- ☐ Vacation
- ☐ Holidays/Floating Holidays
- ☐ Sick/Personal Leave
- ☐ Observance of Special Days
- ☐ Grievance Procedure
- ☐ Special Lunches

D. Discuss Company Philosophy

- ☐ Relationship to Customer/Client
- ☐ Quality Control
- ☐ Use of Facility

E. What Happens at (COMPANY)

- ☐ History of Company
- ☐ Various Departments
- ☐ Products/Services

Continuity of Policies — Right to Change or Discontinue 120

Comment: To allow for maximum flexibility, you should include a concise statement — somewhere in the introduction or first section of your policy manual — which reserves the company's right to change or discontinue policies at any time without notice. Ensure that all employees understand that a policy, once in force, is not irrevocable and can be modified or deleted at anytime. For example, a change in the law might require you to immediately modify or discontinue a policy. The size of your organization and the location of your employees might make it difficult to immediately announce such changes. Therefore, you need to protect the company's rights to make such changes effective without notice.

Give prompt and reasonable notice of any such changes to avoid the problems caused by someone's reliance on a discontinued or modified policy; however, your employees have been forewarned that such changes may occur without notice and will be effective regardless.

Here is a statement you could use or modify to state your right to change or discontinue a policy:

- To preserve the ability to meet company needs under changing conditions, (COMPANY) may modify, augment, delete or revoke any and all policies, procedures, practices, and statements contained in this manual at any time without notice. Such changes shall be effective immediately upon approval by management unless otherwise stated.

If the laws of your state recognize a company handbook or policy manual as a contractual commitment to employees, some stronger, more direct language may avoid such a result in future cases. For example:

- The policies and procedures in this manual are not intended to be contractual commitments by (COMPANY) and they shall not be construed as such by employees. They are intended to be guides to management and merely descriptive of suggested procedures to be followed. (COMPANY) reserves the right to revoke, change, or supplement guidelines at any time without notice. No policy is intended as a guarantee of continuity of benefits or rights. No permanent employment or employment for any term is intended or can be implied by statements in this book.

Acknowledging Receipt of Policy Manual 130

Comment: It is in the company's and employees' best interest to have a sign off sheet for acknowledging receipt of the policy manual. It serves as documentation for the company in case the employee denies having received a copy of the manual or being aware of a particular company policy. For all new employees, this form would be signed, dated, and given to the administrative/personnel office before receipt of his or her first paycheck. You will note in the second sample provided that the employee acknowledges that any future changes in policy will supercede what is written in the manual.

Sample 1

I have received a copy of the (COMPANY) Policy Manual, specifying policies, practices, and regulations, which I agree to observe and follow during my employment with the company. I have read the manual and understand the information contained in it.

______________________________ ______________________________
Employee's Signature Date

Sample 2

I have received my copy of the Policy Manual which outlines the policies, practices, and benefit guidelines of the company, and I have read and I understand the information contained in the Manual.

Since the information in this Manual is necessarily subject to change as situations warrant, it is understood that changes in the manual may supercede, revise, or eliminate one or more of the policies in this manual. These changes will be communicated to me by my supervisor or through official notices. I accept responsibility for keeping informed of these changes.

I further acknowledge my understanding that my employment with (COMPANY) may be terminated at any time with or without cause.

Note: *The preceding sentence should be included only in states where termination at will is permitted and where the employer desires this status.*

______________________________ ______________________________
Employee's Signature Date

____
Name (Please Print)

Chapter 2
Hiring Practices

Introduction

The next section of your policy manual should give the employee an understanding of the process used by the company to recruit, hire, classify, and counsel its employees. The philosophy of the company and the important role played by each employee in the success of the company should continue to unfold in this section. Many of the policies provided in this chapter are regulated by federal statutes, such as Title VII of The Civil Rights Act of 1964, and require frequent updating in order to stay in line with the times, the law, and the competition.

All states have laws and regulations affecting the employee recruitment and selection process. Often these laws and regulations are derived from the applicable federal laws. In some cases, states have additional requirements or broader coverage. You should consult an expert to learn about these differences and reflect them in your policies.

Equal Opportunity 200

Comment: A number of federal and state laws prohibit discrimination in employment and require companies to adopt affirmative action programs. Title VII of the Civil Rights Act of 1964[1] requires that employers with 15 or more employees, who work each workday during any 20 weeks of the current or preceding year, must adhere to the prohibitions against employment discrimination based on race, sex, color, religion, or national origin.

Title VII does not apply to small businesses with fewer than 15 employees; however, there are other federal anti-discrimination laws which do apply to many small businesses. The Civil Rights Act of 1966[2] prohibits discrimination based upon race and national origin. The 1966 Act contains no limitation with respect to number of employees. The Equal Pay Act of 1963[3] prohibits wage differentials based on sex for equal work under similar working conditions. Seniority, merit, or incentive systems are specifically excepted. The Equal Pay Act of 1963 is an amendment to the Fair Labor Standards Act of 1938[4] and covers all employees subject to the FLSA — employers with two or more employees if engaged in commerce or in producing goods for commerce. The Age Discrimination in Employment Act of 1967[5] now prohibits discrimination against employees or applicants who are ages 40 and over. This act is applicable to all employers with 20 or more employees within a 20-week period (similar to the rules under Title VII). The Americans with Disabilities Act of 1990 bars employment discrimination against people with physical or mental disabilities, requires employers to provide reasonable accommodation to the disabled including making existing facilities accessible, to provide special equipment and training, and to arrange part-time or modified work schedules. Accommodations which impose an undue hardship on business operations need not be made. The law applies to employers of 25 or more people by 1992 and by 1994 for employers of 15 or more people.

There are other federal anti-discrimination laws which are applicable to employers who have federal government contracts or subcontracts which are above a certain dollar value — usually relatively low. The major provisions of these laws will be described in any federal government procurement document published to solicit bids, proposals, or quotations.

The anti-discrimination laws relate not only to hiring but also define the employer's obligations regarding compensation, promotion, type of work that may be assigned, and working conditions.

Businesses which may not be covered by these laws should still be aware of their scope. Your business could grow and become subject to the laws. Similarly, states may enact legislation similar to the federal laws and require compliance by small employers as well as large ones.

A word about AIDS: AIDS is a disease which has received a tremendous amount of publicity in the popular media. Employers are concerned about the disease for several reasons; fairness to the AIDS infected employee; impact on employer provided health insurance coverage; and the response of fellow employees. The Federal Centers for Disease Control in Atlanta, Georgia has taken the position that AIDS, while considered contagious, is not casually transmitted.

Most authorities agree that AIDS is a disability or handicap within the framework of the statutes described above. It is to be treated similarly as in the case of other contagious diseases or handicaps. A two-part test should be implemented in the hiring of a disabled or handicapped employee. First, does the applicant have a condition which would prevent the proper performance of the job being applied for? Stated differently, does the employee present a reasonable probability of substantial harm to himself, herself, or others in the workplace? Second, is there a reasonable accommodation which the employer can make to enable the employee to perform the job?

Comparable Worth–Equal Pay: Another issue which impacts the decision to hire and administer salary is the concept of comparable worth or equal pay. Briefly stated, no employer may pay wages to any employee at a rate less than the employer pays employees of the opposite sex for comparable work requiring comparable skills. Both federal and state statutes obligate employers to provide for comparable worth. Failure to do so can result in claims of wage or sex discrimination. Avoidance of these traps requires vigilant monitoring of job classifications — especially ones which seem to be primarily occupied by males or females — and pay scales. This area is also considered in Chapter 3, Compensation.

When developing the company's equal opportunity statement, it may be important to seek legal counsel or consult with federal, state, or local officials to ensure compliance with all statutes and ordinances.

Fetal Protection: The United States Supreme Court has recently ruled that employers may not preclude women of child-bearing age from certain jobs because of a potential risk to their fetuses. These so-called "fetal protection policies" which have been adopted by a number of businesses were held to be discriminatory in violation of Title VII of the 1964 Civil Rights Act.

Equal Opportunity Alternate Policy 1 200.1

Equal Opportunity is (COMPANY) policy. It is our policy to select the best qualified person for each position in the organization. No employee of the company will discriminate against an applicant for employment or a fellow employee because of race, creed, color, religion, sex, national origin, ancestry, age, or other physical or mental handicap. No employee of the company will discriminate against any applicant or fellow employee because of the person's veteran status. This policy applies to all employment practices and personnel actions. (COMPANY) has adopted an affirmative action policy which essentially means that the company will aggressively seek out, hire, develop, and promote qualified members of protected groups (defined as racial minorities, women, physically or mentally handicapped, disabled veterans, veterans of the Vietnam era, and persons ages of 40 and over).

Equal Opportunity Alternate Policy 2 200.2

It is the intent and resolve of (COMPANY) to comply with the requirements and spirit of the law in the implementation of all facets of equal opportunity and affirmative action. In the recruitment, selection, training, utilization, promotion, termination, or any other personnel action, there will be no discrimination on the basis of race, creed, color, religious belief, sex, age, national origin, ancestry, physical or mental handicap, or veteran status. (COMPANY) fully complies with all government requirements for setting up and carrying through affirmative action policies related to the protected classes mentioned above.

It is the responsibility of all managers to see that the company policy of equal opportunity is communicated throughout the organization:

1. A written notice of this policy will be sent to all managers, supervisors, and other employees engaged in employment and training.
2. A copy of our equal opportunity policy will be made available to each new employee or applicant on the first day he or she reports to work or upon request.
3. The company's policy on equal opportunity will be posted in prominent locations.

Recruitment 210

Comment: The recruitment policy statement sets forth the communication process to be followed by your company in filling position requisitions within the organization. It should define the methods of recruitment outside of the organization as well as refer to the in-house requisition posting procedures. The statement should encourage all qualified, present employees to compete for job openings in order to provide employees with an opportunity for upward or lateral mobility and thereby increase morale and save recruitment costs.

A reference statement within the policy should reinforce your company's commitment to equal opportunity and affirmative action. Care should be taken in drafting this policy to avoid the potential for discriminatory recruitment practices (e.g., "word of mouth" or "college" recruitment should not be stated as "preferred" methods). This policy should be evaluated in conjunction with the policy on Employee Selection Process which follows. Again, you may wish to combine the essentials of each policy into one recruitment policy.

Some states impose civil or criminal liability, or both, on an employer who misrepresents working conditions, existence of work, the length of time work will last, compensation for such work, or the status of any strike or labor dispute affecting such work, e.g., California Labor Code, Sections 970–72.

A sample Position Requisition form follows the alternate policy statements on recruitment.

Recruitment Alternate Policy 1 210.1

(COMPANY) leadership position in the business community demands that recruitment consistent with our affirmative action policy be conducted in an aggressive manner to attract top-caliber individuals to fill positions at all levels of the organization. Many positions may be filled by employee transfers or promotions. Others will be assigned to new employees who are recruited or apply directly to the company. Recruitment may be conducted through advertising, employment agencies, schools, employee referrals, or technical and trade referrals. The (VICE PRESIDENT) is the only person who is authorized to approve recruitment funds. Supervisors/managers should discuss the most appropriate method of recruitment for filling departmental positions with the (VICE PRESIDENT). All recruitment shall be conducted in an ethical, professional, and non-discriminatory manner. Before filling any approved position vacancy, current employees who apply shall be given equal consideration for transfer or promotion.

A list of current openings will be posted on all company bulletin boards.

Recruitment Alternate Policy 2 210.2

(COMPANY) provides equal employment opportunity to all applicants on the basis of demonstrated ability, experience, and training. As positions become available within the company, prior to outside recruitment, the (VICE PRESIDENT) and hiring manager shall determine the availability of qualified candidates within the company. Recruitment may be conducted through schools, employment agencies, and company advertising. Contact the (PERSONNEL DIRECTOR) to discuss the most appropriate method of recruitment.

The company bulletin board will display all current openings.

This policy excludes those employed through temporary agencies or "job shops."

EMPLOYMENT OPPORTUNITY/POSITION REQUISITION

Title of Position: ____

Department: ____________________ Classification: Exempt ____ Nonexempt ____

Hiring Supervisor: ____

Reports to: ____

Position Description: ____

____

____

____

Major Job-Related Duties and Functions: ____

____

____

____

Minimum Qualifications: (Knowledge, Skills, Education, and Abilities) ____________________

____

____

____

Additional Desired Qualifications: ____

____

____

____

Employment Status: Regular Full-time ____ Regular Part-time ____ Temporary ____

Salary Range: ____

Potential Career Opportunities in the Position: ____

____

Additional Comments: ____

____

____

____

For additional information, applicants should contact:

____________________	____________________	____________________
Name	Telephone	Date

Employee Selection Process 220

Comment: The Employee Selection Process policy statement establishes the authority and responsibility of designated management staff in the selection function. Its design should minimize your company's efforts and maximize its resources in selecting the best candidate available for an open position. The policy should provide assurance of your company's intention to recruit, hire, place, promote, and transfer for all positions without regard to race, religion, color, national origin, sex, age, or physical handicap, except where physical fitness is a valid occupational qualification.

In developing this policy, consideration should be given to recent innovations. Some companies provide cash awards or other incentives to employees who seek and refer applicants who are subsequently hired. For example, a nonexempt position filled in this way may carry a $100 bonus. An exempt, professional, or executive position may carry a $300 bonus. Other incentives include a day or two off with pay or use of the company condominium for a weekend. The recruitment cost savings is obvious; however, a word of caution is appropriate. Such an incentive system may result in word of mouth recruiting becoming a preferred or sole method of recruiting. This may lead to a charge of discriminatory hiring practices being leveled at the company, if there is a lack of minority and female candidates, even though management's intent is benign.

The Immigration Reform and Control Act of 1986 (a.k.a. the Simpson–Rodino Act) makes a notable impact on most employers' recruitment and selection policies and procedures. The law prohibits employers, who hire four or more employees, from employment discrimination based on national origin or citizenship. A major burden on employers is the (1) prohibition against knowingly hiring, or continuing to hire, illegal aliens; (2) verification measures required; and (3) the maintenance of records showing the immigration status and certifications required by the law and implementing regulations.

Basically, the immigration status of all new hires must be verified by the examination of documents or records showing both employment and identity. A U.S. passport or a green card satisfies both the employment authorization and identity requirements. Otherwise, both an employment authorization record, such as a Social Security card and U.S. birth certificate, and an identity document, such as a U.S. drivers license or identity card, must be examined. The documents must appear to be genuine to a reasonable person.

The employer must attest in writing under penalty of perjury that the employer saw the documentation. Also, the employee attests, again in writing and under penalty of perjury, that he or she is authorized to work in the United States. These attestations are made on *Form I–9, Employment Eligibility Verification*, which must be kept by the employer for three years after recruitment or for at least one year after the employee's termination, whichever occurs last. A list of the authorized documents or records and *Form I–9* may be obtained from the Immigration and Naturalization Department. A sample of *Form I–9* for both employer and employee certifications is at the end of the alternative policies.

The law does not require you to maintain photocopies of the documents that you have examined; however, the practice is permitted by the law and is evidence of a good faith attempt to comply, which is a defense to a charge of employing an illegal alien. Hiring, recruiting, continuing to employ, or referring for hire an alien who is not authorized to work in the United States is punishable by civil fines — a $250 minimum fine up to a $10,000 maximum fine for a third offense for each alien. A pattern or practice of violations is a criminal matter (up to six months in jail or a $3,000 fine, or both, for each alien). The Act also extends to independent contractors and employment policies.

A sample Interview Summary Sheet follows the alternate policy statements.

Employee Selection Process Alternate Policy 1 220.1

Selection of candidates for all positions will follow (COMPANY) Equal Opportunity and Affirmative Action policies. The vice president is responsible for preparing the position requisition. Only the (VICE PRESIDENT) is authorized to place ads, respond to inquiries from employment agencies, and post requisitions on the company bulletin boards.

Job-related duties and qualifications, as listed on the position requisition, will provide the basis for initial screening of applications. All applications and resumés received for the requisitioned position will be forwarded to the vice president. Initial screening for the minimum qualifications will be conducted by the vice president. The vice president will further screen the applications to select those individuals to be interviewed for the position. Only job-related questions or ones which assess the candidate's experience, skill, and training will be asked. Definite salary commitments will be avoided during the initial interview.

Some positions will require skills for which a known level of competence must exist, for example, typing, mathematics, and keypunch. Under these circumstances, applicants may be asked to demonstrate these skills by completing an exercise involving a job-related work sample. It must be evident that such an exercise measures knowledge or skills required for the particular job. The results of an exercise must prove to be a valid prediction of job performance. All interviewed applicants must be given the same exercise.

The vice president will be responsible for verification of employment information provided by the applicant, if the information is needed in making a candidate selection. The only information to be verified from prior employers will be the following:

1. Dates of employment

Employee Selection Process — continued Alternate Policy 1 220.1

2. Positions held

3. Salary at time of termination

The applicant should be advised that this information will be verified. Additional information should not be requested from prior employers, unless the applicant agrees in writing, because it may violate the applicant's privacy.

Every newly-hired employee must verify their eligibility for employment within three business days of accepting employment. The vice president will not notify other candidates that the position has been filled until the new employee has complied with the law. The employee will fill out and execute the top of *Form I-9 (see sample at end of Alternate Policy 2)*. The vice president will complete *Form I–9* after examining the employee's documentation of identity and employment eligibility. Each document examined will be photocopied and the copy maintained in the employee's personnel file folder.

Employee Selection Process Alternate Policy 2 220.2

(COMPANY) provides equal opportunity to all applicants on the basis of demonstrated ability, experience, training, and potential. Qualified persons are selected without prejudice or discrimination as stated in the company's Equal Opportunity and Affirmative Action policies.

The employment requisitions, initiated by the (VICE PRESIDENT), will define the job-related tasks and qualifications necessary to assume the position. The defined tasks and stated qualifications will be the basis for screening applications. The (VICE PRESIDENT) will conduct structured initial interviews limited to job-related questions to assess the candidates' experience, demonstrated ability, and training. The telephone may be used for these initial interviews. Pre-employment tests demonstrated to be job-relevant and valid according to accepted professional practices may be used. Such tests are to be administered only by trained personnel in the prescribed professional manner. All interviewed applicants will be asked to take the test.

Before extending an employment offer and upon the applicant's prior agreement that inquiries may be made, at least two applicant references must be checked. Inquiries are to be made in a professional manner requesting only factually verifiable and job-related information. The reference data is used only as supplemental information for the hiring decision.

Following employment, the information will be retained for one year before being destroyed.

Note: *Check your state law for records retention requirements.*

After candidate interviews, verification of employment history, and reference inquiries, the vice president is responsible for the employment offer. The vice president may make the offer personally or may delegate this responsibility to another company officer.

Employee Selection Process — continued Alternate Policy 2 220.2

After the verbal offer has been made and the candidate has agreed to the essential terms of the offer (typically position, employee classification, salary or rate, and starting date), a written offer will be prepared and submitted to the candidate in person or by mail. The written offer will confirm the verbal offer and will include the essential terms of the verbal offer as agreed to by the candidate. The candidate will be required to sign and date an acceptance of the written offer which will state as follows: "The undersigned accepts the above employment offer and agrees that it contains the terms of employment with (COMPANY) and that there are no other terms express or implied. It is understood that employment is subject to verification of identity and employment eligibility and may be terminated by the (COMPANY) at any time for any reason."

The verbal or written offer must never express or imply that employment is "permanent," "long-term," of a specific duration, or words of similar meaning. An exception may be made where a temporary position of known duration is to be filled. Employment may be made contingent upon certain job-related factors, such as obtaining a specific state or federal license or security clearance when appropriate or desirable.

Once the candidate has accepted the employment offer, she or he will be required to provide documentation of identity and employment eligibility in accordance with federal law. The *Form I–9* (a copy of which is included at the end of this policy) shall be used for this purpose.

INTERVIEW SUMMARY SHEET

Applicant's Name ________________________________ Date ____________

Position ________________________ Interviewer ________________________

Qualifications (taken from job announcement): ________________________

Applicant's Background: ________________________

Job Functions:

Skills: ________________________

Education: ________________________

Knowledge: ________________________

Applicant's Experience: ________________________

References of Previous Supervisors or Managers: ________________________

Preferred Qualifications: ________________________

Personal Factors: ________________________

Growth in Career: ________________________

Accomplishments: ________________________

Applicant's Strengths: ________________________

Applicant's Limitations: ________________________

Interviewer Comments: ________________________

EMPLOYMENT ELIGIBILITY VERIFICATION (Form I-9)

1 **EMPLOYEE INFORMATION AND VERIFICATION:** (To be completed and signed by employee.)

Name: (Print or Type) Last	First	Middle	Birth Name
Address: Street Name and Number	City	State	ZIP Code
Date of Birth (Month Day Year)		Social Security Number	

I attest, under penalty of perjury, that I am (check a box):

☐ 1. A citizen or national of the United States.

☐ 2. An alien lawfully admitted for permanent residence (Alien Number A ____________________).

☐ 3. An alien authorized by the Immigration and Naturalization Service to work in the United States (Alien Number A ____________________ , or Admission Number ____________________ , expiration of employment authorization, if any ____________________).

I attest, under penalty of perjury, the documents that I have presented as evidence of identity and employment eligibility are genuine and relate to me. I am aware that federal law provides for imprisonment and/or fine for any false statements or use of false documents in connection with this certificate.

Signature	Date (Month/Day/Year)

PREPARER TRANSLATOR CERTIFICATION (To be completed if prepared by person other than the employee) I attest, under penalty of perjury, that the above was prepared by me at the request of the named individual and is based on all information of which I have any knowledge.

Signature	Name (Print or Type)		
Address (Street Name and Number)	City	State	Zip Code

2 **EMPLOYER REVIEW AND VERIFICATION:** (To be completed and signed by employer.)

Instructions:

Examine one document from List A and check the appropriate box, ***OR*** examine one document from List B ***and*** one from List C and check the appropriate boxes.

Provide the ***Document Identification Number*** and ***Expiration Date*** for the document checked.

List A
Documents that Establish Identity and Employment Eligibility

☐ 1. United States Passport

☐ 2. Certificate of United States Citizenship

☐ 3. Certificate of Naturalization

☐ 4. Unexpired foreign passport with attached Employment Authorization

☐ 5. Alien Registration Card with photograph

Document Identification

\# ____________________

Expiration Date (if any)

____

List B
Documents that Establish Identity

and

☐ 1. A State-issued driver's license or a State-issued I.D. card with a photograph, or information, including name, sex, date of birth, height, weight, and color of eyes.
(Specify State)____________________)

☐ 2. U.S. Military Card

☐ 3. Other (Specify document and issuing authority)

____

Document Identification

\# ____________________

Expiration Date (if any)

____

List C
Documents that Establish Employment Eligibility

☐ 1. Original Social Security Number Card (other than a card stating it is not valid for employment)

☐ 2. A birth certificate issued by State, county, or municipal authority bearing a seal or other certification

☐ 3. Unexpired INS Employment Authorization Specify form
\# ____________________

Document Identification

\# ____________________

Expiration Date (if any)

____

CERTIFICATION: I attest, under penalty of perjury, that I have examined the documents presented by the above individual, that they appear to be genuine and to relate to the individual named, and that the individual, to the best of my knowledge, is eligible to work in the United States.

Signature	Name (Print or Type)	Title
Employer Name	Address	Date

Employment Eligibility Verification

NOTICE: Authority for collecting the information on this form is in Title 8, United States Code, Section 1324A, which requires employers to verify employment eligibility of individuals on a form approved by the Attorney General. This form will be used to verify the individual's eligibility for employment in the United States. Failure to present this form for inspection to officers of the Immigration and Naturalization Service or Department of Labor within the time period specified by regulation, or improper completion or retention of this form, may be a violation of the above law and may result in a civil money penalty.

Section 1. Instructions to Employee/Preparer for completing this form

Instructions for the employee.

All employees, upon being hired, must complete Section 1 of this form. Any person hired after November 6, 1986 must complete this form. (For the purpose of completion of this form the term "hired" applies to those employed, recruited or referred for a fee.)

All employees must print or type their complete name, address, date of birth, and Social Security Number. The block which correctly indicates the employee's immigration status must be checked. If the second block is checked, the employee's Alien Registration Number must be provided. If the third block is checked, the employee's Alien Registration Number ***or*** Admission Number must be provided, as well as the date of expiration of that status, if it expires.

All employees whose present names differ from birth names, because of marriage or other reasons, must print or type their birth names in the appropriate space of Section 1. Also, employees whose names change after employment verification should report these changes to their employer.

All employees must sign and date the form.

Instructions for the preparer of the form, if not the employee.

If a person assists the employee with completing this form, the preparer must certify the form by signing it and printing or typing his or her complete name and address.

Section 2. Instructions to Employer for completing this form

(For the purpose of completion of this form, the term "employer" applies to employers and those who recruit or refer for a fee.)

Employers must complete this section by examining evidence of identity and employment eligibility, and:

- checking the appropriate box in List A ***or*** boxes in both Lists B and C;
- recording the document identification number and expiration date (if any);
- recording the type of form if not specifically identified in the list;
- signing the certification section.

NOTE: Employers are responsible for reverifying employment eligibility of employees whose employment eligibility documents carry an expiration date.

Copies of documentation presented by an individual for the purpose of establishing identity and employment eligibility may be copied and retained for the purpose of complying with the requirements of this form and no other purpose. Any copies of documentation made for this purpose should be maintained with this form.

Name changes of employees which occur after preparation of this form should be recorded on the form by lining through the old name, printing the new name and the reason (such as marriage), and dating and initialing the changes. Employers should not attempt to delete or erase the old name in any fashion.

RETENTION OF RECORDS.

The completed form must be retained by the employer for:

- three years after the date of hiring; or
- one year after the date the employment is terminated, whichever is later.

Employers may photocopy or reprint this form as necessary.

U.S. Department of Justice
Immigration and Naturalization Service

OMB #1115-0136
Form I-9 (05/07/87)

Smoking 230

Comment: After years of quietly accepting cigarette smoking as an inevitable part of the work environment, many health-conscious individuals are responsible for a change of attitude toward smoking both in public and, particularly, on the job.

Research over the past few years indicates:

- Absenteeism is higher for smokers than nonsmokers;
- Smokers have more accidents than nonsmokers because they pay less attention to their work while smoking;
- Productivity among smokers is lower because they spend time smoking;
- Estimated costs to the company for each smoking employee range from $650 to $3,500 for a variety of reasons, including workers' compensation, janitorial service costs, damage to office furniture and draperies, and insurance claims.

Of course, the impact of smoking is not limited to smokers themselves. Employers have to consider the possibility that nonsmoking employees and customers will complain because of exposure to smokers in the workplace. As nonsmokers become more demonstrative about their needs, smokers demand equal rights. What is an employer to do to preserve harmony in the workplace? Obviously, this issue calls for a policy. In some places, notably San Francisco, certain employers are required to have a policy by law. Many municipalities have also enacted ordinances in this area.

As the policy is developed, consider the impact it will have on present employees who do smoke. Much of the dissatisfaction among present employees can be avoided if they are involved in deciding the necessary restrictions. Since health and safety are so closely linked in the discussion of smoking, you will want to reinforce this in your policy. Consider:

- The exact nature of the hazards of smoking to your particular type of business;
- The effect of smoking on the smoker as well as the co-workers; and
- The impact of smoking on productivity.

Include the company's rationale for the policy in the policy itself. Define areas in which smoking is forbidden, as well as permitted, and the disciplinary action to be taken if the policy is violated. You don't have to preach to your employees about the evil of smoking, but you do have the duty to create a healthy-working atmosphere where everyone's rights are respected.

Smoking Alternate Policy 1 230.1

No smoking will be allowed in the office area at any time. This policy is for the health and safety of all employees. Smoking will be allowed only in the lunchroom, restrooms, and designated areas.

Your cooperation is requested, as this policy must be rigidly enforced to comply with the company health and safety requirements and to maintain proper insurance coverage for our building.

Smoking Alternate Policy 2 230.2

With the wide variation in space, ventilation, and general physical arrangements within (COMPANY) departments, a single policy cannot be established for the entire company. Each vice president, with the cooperation of smokers and nonsmokers alike, will establish a department smoking policy regarding the following points: (1) separation of smokers and nonsmokers in the department; (2) the policy regarding smoking during any group meetings; and (3) the purchase of air purification equipment by employees, if necessary.

Each department policy will be clearly posted in the work area. All new employees will be given a copy of the policy and if a conflict arises, the supervisor will resolve it in accord with department policies and good judgment.

Smoking Alternate Policy 3 230.3

Because the smoking of tobacco or any other weed or plant is a danger to health and is a cause of material annoyance and discomfort to those who are present in confined places, (COMPANY) hereby declares the purposes of this policy are (1) to protect the public health and welfare by regulating smoking in the office workplace; and (2) to minimize the toxic effects of smoking in the office workplace by adopting a policy that will accommodate, insofar as possible, the preferences of nonsmokers and smokers alike. If a satisfactory accommodation cannot be reached, smoking will be prohibited in the office workplace. This policy is not intended to create any right to smoke.

For purposes of this policy, the following definitions shall apply.

1. "Employee" means any person who is employed by (COMPANY) in return for direct or indirect monetary wages or profit;

2. "Office Workplace" means any enclosed area of a structure or portion of the company premises. Office workplace includes, but is not limited to, office spaces in office buildings, waiting rooms, and libraries.

3. "Smoking" or "to smoke" means and includes inhaling, exhaling, burning, or carrying any lighted smoking equipment for tobacco or any other weed or plant; and

4. "Enclosed" means closed in by a roof and four walls with appropriate openings for entrances and exits and is not intended to mean areas commonly described as public lobbies.

Any nonsmoking employee may object to his or her vice president about smoke in his or her workplace. Using already available means of ventilation or separation or partition

▶

Smoking — continued Alternate Policy 3 230.3

of office space, the supervisor or manager shall attempt to reach a reasonable accommodation, insofar as possible, between the preferences of nonsmoking and smoking employees. However, the company is not required to make any expenditures or structural changes to accommodate the preferences of nonsmoking or smoking employees.

If an accommodation which is satisfactory to all affected nonsmoking employees cannot be reached in any given office workplace, the preferences of nonsmoking employees shall prevail and smoking shall be prohibited in that office workplace. Where (COMPANY) prohibits smoking in an office workplace, the area in which smoking is prohibited shall be clearly marked with signs.

The Smoking Policy shall be posted conspicuously in all workplaces and shall be given in writing to every prospective employee and new hire.

Every vice president who has questions or issues regarding implementation of this policy is requested to contact the (VICE PRESIDENT) for guidance and interpretation.

Smoking Alternate Policy 4 230.4

With the current evidence that smoking is dangerous and injurious to a person's health, employees are encouraged not to smoke; however, (COMPANY) recognizes that the decision to smoke or not to smoke is a personal one. During working hours, our policy is to limit smoking to the restrooms, lunchroom, and in certain designated areas. Check with your supervisor.

Employment Classifications 240

Comment: Most positions within any company are thought to require fulltime employees. Employment classifications should be defined to provide supervisors/managers with a guide in determining other alternatives in the selection of employees to meet company needs. The classifications will also be used by the personnel department and accounting in recordkeeping.

Two alternative employment status definitions are provided on the following pages. The work hours are given as an example and may not fit all companies — some companies have a 35- or 37.5- hour workweek.

Caution: The authors recommend that you do not use "permanent" or similar language in classifications. The use of this language may affect your right to discharge employees "at will." See the **Comment** portion of Section 295, Terminations, which is mentioned later in this chapter.

Collective bargaining agreements between an employer and a labor union representing an employer's employees may provide for additional classifications. Similarly, other provisions of a personnel policy manual may be superseded by inconsistent portions of the policy manual at least insofar as union employees covered by a collective bargaining agreement are concerned.

An Employee Hiring Confirmation Form follows the alternate policies on employee classifications. This form provides an audit trail for personnel in processing the payroll.

Employment Classifications Alternate Policy 1 240.1

There are three classifications of employees:

1. Regular Fulltime — An employee who works a normal 40-hour workweek on a regularly-scheduled basis.
2. Regular Part-time — An employee who works less than a normal workweek, on either a regularly-scheduled basis or on an irregular basis.
3. Temporary — An employee hired for a period not exceeding three months and who is not entitled to regular benefits. An extension of a temporary work classification for an additional three-month period, or less, may be granted, if upon review by management, the assignment is clearly found to be necessary. A temporary employee may be fulltime or part-time. In addition to the use of this classification for secretarial or clerical positions, it applies to students who work during the summer.

All employees are classified as exempt and nonexempt according to these definitions:

Salaried Exempt — Positions of a managerial, administrative, or professional nature or for outside sales, as prescribed by federal and state labor statutes, which are exempt from mandatory overtime payments.

Salaried Nonexempt — Positions of a clerical, technical, or service nature, as defined by statute, which are covered by provisions for overtime payments.

Note: *These definitions are illustrative in nature and are not intended as a statement of the law. Refer to the* **Comment** *preceding the policy on Overtime Compensation, Section 350, the Fair Labor Standards Act, and applicable state law.*

If you are uncertain as to your status, please contact your vice president.

Employment Classifications Alternate Policy 2 240.2

Positions within the company are generally designed to require fulltime employees. In certain functions and during some seasons, work schedules and company needs may require the services of other than fulltime employees. There are four classifications of employees at (COMPANY):

1. Fulltime — An employee hired for an indefinite period in a position for which the normal work schedule is 40 hours per week.

2. Part-time — An employee hired for an indefinite period in a position for which the normal work schedule is at least 20 but less than 40 hours per week.

3. Temporary — An employee hired for a position for which the scheduled workweek can range from less than 20 to 40 hours, but the position is required for only a specific, known duration, usually less than six months.

4. Summer — An employee hired only for the summer months (typically June through September) for a position for which the scheduled workweek can range from less than 20 to 40 hours.

Neither temporary nor summer employees qualify for regular company benefits.

Provisions in the Fair Labor Standards Act divide all employees into two categories, exempt and nonexempt, with respect to eligibility for overtime payment. They shall be defined as:

Exempt — An employee considered to be either managerial, administrative, professional or outside sales.

▶

Employment Classifications — continued Alternate Policy 2 240.2

Nonexempt — An employee who devotes most of his or her hours in activities that are not managerial, administrative, professional or outside sales.

Note: *These definitions are illustrative in nature and are not intended as a statement of the law. Refer to the* **Comment** *preceding the policy on Overtime Compensation, Section 350, the Fair Labor Standards Act, and applicable state law.*

If you are uncertain as to your status, please contact your vice president.

EMPLOYEE HIRING CONFIRMATION

Name of Employee ______________________

Department ______________________

Position ______________________

Job Description attached ______________________

Proposed Start Date ______________

Rate of Pay ______________________

Employment Classification

- ☐ 1. Regular full-time
- ☐ 2. Regular part-time # hours per week __________
- ☐ 3. Temporary # of weeks/months __________

	Day		Lunch	
Proposed Work Hours -	Start	__________	Start	__________
	Stop	__________	Stop	__________

Probationary Period __________ days

Remarks/Special Conditions: ______________________________________

____

____

____

Special health or working condition requirements: ______________________

____

____

____

____
Supervisor's Signature

____
Employee's Signature

Anniversary Date and Reinstatement 250

Comment: In defining an employee's anniversary date, there are several dates that might be considered:

- The first day on the job,
- The date the employment offer is accepted by the applicant, or
- The date he or she signs the necessary company employment documents.

In making the decision as to which date to choose as the anniversary date, consider the effect the date will have on the company's benefit programs, such as insurance or pension plan. It also should be easily interpreted by management and other employees. Naturally, the same date should be used for all employees, but the choice is important because employee morale and recordkeeping will be affected if your company has to change in midstream. The policy statement provided for consideration can easily be rewritten to reflect your company's decision on any of the three possible anniversary dates mentioned above or any others chosen.

Your company will want to determine the effect an employee's termination and later re-employment will have on that employee's anniversary date because of benefits related to time employed with the company. Reinstatement to the original anniversary date may imply some kind of "permanent" employment which may affect your right to discharge an employee later. From the perspective of morale; however, it is worthwhile to accept this risk. With regard to pension or retirement plans and striking employees, legal counsel should be consulted to determine if Alternative Policy 2 complies with the current law. Arguably it does, at least with respect to strikes, because striking employees generally cannot be "terminated" but only "replaced." Retirement plans often provide for reinstatement of a terminated employee's vested status if the employee is reinstated within one year following termination. In such event, an additional sentence should be added to the policy manual stating, "In the event of any inconsistency between this policy manual and any retirement plan maintained by the company, the terms and conditions of the retirement plan shall prevail."

Anniversary Date Alternate Policy 1 250.1

An employee's anniversary date is defined as his or her first day on the job with the company. Performance reviews will be completed annually on the employee's anniversary date. Although a salary adjustment never automatically follows a performance review, if a review cannot be completed prior to the employee's anniversary date and a salary adjustment is in order, it will be made retroactive to the anniversary date.

Note: *The last two sentences are optional and can be omitted by the company that wants to specify periodic evaluation dates in a separate policy.*

Reinstatement Alternate Policy 2 250.2

Employees who are reinstated into the company will maintain their original anniversary date for seniority purposes as well as for those benefit programs governed by the anniversary date. The policy will be as follows:

1. Layoff — Employees who terminate because of reduction in work force will maintain their original anniversary date for seniority purposes, if they are re-employed by (COMPANY) within one year after date of termination.

2. Voluntary resignation — Employees who voluntarily terminate their employment with (COMPANY) may maintain their original anniversary date, subject to management approval, if they are re-employed by the company within six months after date of termination. The company is under no obligation to rehire any such employee.

Reinstatement Alternate Policy 3 250.3

Employees who are re-employed by the company after termination will lose their original anniversary date for all purposes and be assigned a new date corresponding to their first day on the job after re-employment. This policy shall not apply to layoffs or to an employee who was erroneously terminated for cause and later reinstated.

New Hire, Rehire, Relatives, and Return to Work After Serious Injury or Illness 260–80

Comment: The policy statements contained in the following sections define the consistent procedures to be followed by your company concerning the orientation of new hires, the processing of rehires, and the employment of relatives of present employees. Also included in the policy statement is the procedure to be followed for those employees who have been absent from work because of an injury or extended illness. With the exception of the policy on Relatives, alternate policies are not provided.

Caution must be exercised to avoid policies which restrict the hiring of spouses. Such policies may be deemed to discriminate because of sex. Similarly, a policy which seeks to bar employment of persons who are spouses of persons employed by a competitor may also be discriminatory. A policy restricting the hiring of family members employed by the company or a competitor would seem to remove the discriminatory taint, but legal counsel should be consulted prior to drafting this policy in any event.

For your convenience, the above issues have been segregated into separate policies to enable you to pick and choose policies for your manual. With only minor modifications, these policies can be combined to form one policy.

New Hire 260.1

The (VICE PRESIDENT) is responsible for having the new employee fill out all pre-employment forms, benefit applications, and enrollment forms; having his or her picture taken for the company identification card; and providing, on the employee's first day of work, basic information on pay and leave policies, benefits, parking situations, and working hours. Within the first week of employment, a new employee orientation will be conducted by the (VICE PRESIDENT).

Note: *Delete the last sentence if your company has no structured orientation meeting.*

Rehire 265.1

Applications received from former employees will be processed using the same procedures and standards that govern all direct applications. The vice president will review the former employee's performance records and the circumstances surrounding termination of previous employment with the company. This information will be provided to the staff responsible for screening and interviewing applicants. (COMPANY) is under no obligation to rehire former employees.

Relatives Alternate Policy 1 270.1

(COMPANY) permits the hiring of relatives of current employees, if the applicant is qualified and selected by the hiring manager/supervisor. The primary consideration for placement is the proximity of the relatives' work areas to each other. Only in extraordinary circumstances, with management approval, should an employee be directly or indirectly supervised by a relative. A relative is defined as any person related to the employee by blood, marriage, or adoption.

Relatives Alternate Policy 2 270.2

Relatives of (COMPANY) employees may apply and, if qualified, will be considered for employment except in certain sensitive areas, such as accounting, personnel, or research and development. Relatives will not be allowed to supervise or evaluate each other. Relatives will not work in the same department or under the same supervisor or manager. A relative is defined as any person related to the employee by blood, marriage, or adoption in the following degrees: parent, child, grandparent, grandchild; brother, sister, brother-in-law, sister-in-law; aunt, uncle, niece, nephew; and first cousin.

Relatives Alternate Policy 3 270.3

It is the policy of (COMPANY) not to hire relatives of current employees or relatives of persons employed by competitors of the company.

Return to Work After Serious Injury or Illness 280.1

As a joint protection to the employee and the company, employees who have been absent from work because of serious illness or injury are required to obtain a doctor's release specifically stating that the employee is capable of performing his or her normal duties or assignments. A serious injury or illness is defined as one that results in the employee being absent from work for more than (ADD NUMBER) consecutive weeks, or one which may limit the employee's future performance of regular duties or assignments.

(COMPANY) management shall ensure that employees who return to work after a serious injury or illness are physically capable of performing their duties or assignments without risk of reinjury or relapse.

If the cause of the employee's illness or injury was job-related, the employee's vice president will make every reasonable effort to assign the returning employee to assignments consistent with the instructions of the employee's doctor until the employee is fully recovered. A doctor's written release is required before recovery can be assumed.

Performance Improvement 290

Comment: This policy establishes a consistent program of progressive actions to help your employees and their supervisors discuss and resolve performance deficiencies or employee misconduct. If an employee's performance or conduct is not meeting the company's standards, he or she should be given adequate time and guidance to improve performance or conduct. For a small business, it is usually the vice president who assumes direct responsibility for counseling and guiding the employee.

Care should be taken in drafting a policy of this kind for several reasons. Proven major violations of company policies or gross misconduct — fraudulent expense reports, stealing company property, or substantial conflicts of interest — may lead to immediate suspension or discharge. This policy should be drafted to give management the sole discretion in deciding the appropriate level of discipline without having to resort to a structured, unyielding process of successive steps before discharge for major violations. In addition, the time and expense required to administer a highly structured review or counseling process, or both, may prove unduly burdensome for smaller employers.

Recent court cases, notably in California and Michigan, have begun to erode the right of an employer to discharge at will. While it is beyond the scope of this book to summarize and evaluate these recent cases and the legal theories involved, remember that company policies are statements of rules and sometimes rights. To the extent employees are granted rights by company policies, or are erroneously led to believe that they have certain rights, the courts may likely recognize those rights in much the same way as courts recognize contractual rights and corresponding duties. Indeed, some courts look upon written, or consistently applied verbal policies, as forming part of a contractual relationship between employer and employee.

To the extent that you have created a policy with a structured process of successive steps, or provide for some kind of an appeal procedure, you should follow it to the letter. If you make exceptions to the process for certain employees, without reserving the right to do so in the policy itself, your exceptions may be viewed as a breach of contract or a modification to your stated policies.

Language has been incorporated into the first paragraph of the following policy which provides management with the flexibility necessary to avoid a structured process. It also reserves the right to disregard this policy and discharge at will when appropriate to do so. Companies desiring to maintain the structured process can remove the at will language and redraft this policy accordingly.

Another alternative to consider when deciding between flexibility and structure is to adopt two separate policies, one for performance improvement and a second for misconduct. The former expresses a confidence that the employee can improve his or her performance through the guidance and assistance of management. The latter is reserved for those cases where discipline must be used to discourage employees from inappropriate behavior. Another common error to avoid is the long or short list of violations which may lead to some type of disciplinary action. To the extent that you try to specifically define and prohibit all types of misconduct, you may be limiting management's prerogatives rather than enhancing them. No list can be all-inclusive, and it may be considered exclusive unless you state that the list is for purposes of example only and not exclusive.

Other companies may choose to disregard the following policy entirely in order to avoid the issues discussed here. Although this is acceptable, consideration should be given to two points. First, management should conspicuously state its right to discharge at will. It would be better to have several consistent references to this right in several different policies or company communications. Second, a performance improvement policy is a method to preserve the company's costly investment of time and training (and save future recruiting expenses) in an employee who should be given reasonable guidance and time to become a more efficient and productive person.

One other characteristic of the policy that follows is its emphasis that all corrective or disciplinary action be documented. Every employer should make documentation mandatory. Such documentation is extremely important, possibly as evidence, and certainly to refresh a supervisor's or manager's recollection of events that led to the discharge of an employee for cause. Some employees, although discharged for proven cause, may feel justified in filing a claim for unemployment compensation or an administrative claim or lawsuit alleging discrimination or a wrongful discharge under various legal theories. In these situations, one of the first things a state agency or the attorneys will want to examine is the former employee's personnel file. It is better to be slightly overprepared than underprepared. Once documented, great care must be taken to preserve the file and its contents. All information pertaining to the employee, whether positive or negative, should be kept in his or her personnel file. Incomplete, missing or "doctored" files or records will almost certainly cause a company more harm than a completed, well-maintained file.

The authors recommend that before drafting your Performance Improvement policy you also read the **Comment** and policies on Terminations, which immediately follows this section.

Performance Improvement 290.1

Performance improvement may be suggested when company management believes that an employee's performance is less than satisfactory and can be resolved through adequate counseling. Corrective counseling is completely at the discretion of company management. The company desires to protect its investment of time and expense devoted to employee orientation and training whenever that goal is in the company's best interests. The company expressly reserves the right to discharge "at will." Even if corrective counseling is implemented, it may be terminated at the discretion of management. Management, in its sole discretion, may either warn, reassign, suspend, or discharge any employee at will, whichever it chooses and at any time.

The (VICE PRESIDENT), will determine the course of action best suited to the circumstances. The steps in performance improvement are as follows:

1. Verbal counseling — As the first step in correcting unacceptable performance or behavior, the vice president should review pertinent job requirements with the employee to ensure his or her understanding of them. The vice president should consider the severity of the problem, the employee's previous performance appraisals and all of the circumstances surrounding the particular case. The seriousness of the performance or misconduct should be indicated by stating that a written warning, probation, or possible termination could result if the problem is not resolved. The employee should be asked to review what has been discussed to ensure his or her understanding of the seriousness of the problem and the corrective action necessary. The vice president should document the verbal counseling for future reference immediately following the review.

▶

Performance Improvement — continued 290.1

2. Written counseling — If the unacceptable performance or behavior continues, the next step should be a written warning. Certain circumstances, such as violation of a widely known policy or safety requirement, may justify a written warning without first using verbal counseling. The written warning defines the problem and how it may be corrected. The seriousness of the problem is again emphasized, and the written warning shall indicate that probation or termination or both, may result if improvement is not observed. Written counseling becomes part of the employee's personnel file, although the vice president may direct that the written warning be removed after a period of time, under appropriate circumstances.

3. Probation — If the problem has not been resolved through written counseling or the circumstances warrant it, or both, the individual should be placed on probation. Probation is a serious action in which the employee is advised that termination will occur if improvement in performance or conduct is not achieved within the probationary period.

   The (VICE PRESIDENT), after review of the employee's corrective counseling documentation, will determine the length of probation. Typically, the probation period should be at least two weeks and no longer than 60 days, depending on the circumstances. A written probationary notice to the employee is prepared by the vice president. The letter should include a statement of the following:

   - The specific unsatisfactory situation;
   - A review of oral and written warnings;
   - The length of probation;
   - The specific behavior modification or acceptable level of performance;
   - Suggestions for improvement;

▶

Performance Improvement — continued 290.1

- A scheduled counseling session or sessions during the probationary period;
- A statement that further action, including termination, may result if defined improvement or behavior modification does not result during probation. "Further action" may include, but is not limited to reassignment, reduction in pay, grade, or demotion.

The vice president should personally meet with the employee to discuss the probationary letter and answer any questions. The employee should acknowledge receipt by signing the letter. If the employee should refuse to sign, the vice president may sign attesting that it was delivered to the employee and identifying the date of delivery. The probationary letter becomes part of the employee's personnel file.

On the defined probation counseling date or dates, the employee and vice president will meet to review the employee's progress in correcting the problem which led to the probation. Brief written summaries of these meetings should be prepared with copies provided to the employee and the (VICE PRESIDENT).

At the completion of the probationary period, the (VICE PRESIDENT) and the employee will meet to determine whether the employee has achieved the required level of performance and to consider removing the employee from probation, extending the period of probation, or taking further action. The employee is to be advised in writing of the decision. Should probation be completed successfully, the employee should be commended, though cautioned that any future recurrence may result in further disciplinary action.

4. Suspension — A two or three day suspension without pay may be justified when circumstances reasonably require an investigation of a serious incident in which the employee was allegedly involved. A suspension may also be warranted when employee

▶

Performance Improvement — continued 290.1

safety, welfare, or morale may be adversely affected if a suspension is not imposed. In addition, and with prior approval of the (VICE PRESIDENT), suspension without pay for up to three consecutive working days may be imposed for such proven misconduct as intentional violation of safety rules, fighting, or drinking alcohol on the job. These examples do not limit management's use of suspension with or without pay in other appropriate circumstances, such as the need to investigate a serious incident. In implementing a suspension, a written counseling report should set forth the circumstances justifying the suspension. Such a report shall become part of the employee's personnel file.

Note: *Suspension is a disciplinary action and is not normally reserved for performance deficiencies.*

5. Involuntary Termination — The involuntary termination notice is prepared by the vice president. The employee is notified of the termination by the vice president and will be directed to report to the vice president for debriefing and completion of termination documentation. Involuntary termination is reserved for those cases that cannot be resolved by corrective counseling or in those cases where a major violation has occurred which cannot be tolerated.

   Note: *Those companies that desire to maximize flexibility and preserve the right to discharge at will should delete this last sentence and the remainder of this policy.*

The following definitions and classification of violations, for which corrective counseling, performance improvement, or other disciplinary action may be taken, are merely illustrative and not limited to these examples. A particular violation may be major or minor, depending on the surrounding facts or circumstances.

▶

Performance Improvement — continued 290.1

1. Minor violations — Less serious violations that have some effect on the continuity, efficiency of work, safety, and harmony within the company. They typically lead to corrective counseling unless repeated or when unrelated incidents occur in rapid succession. Here are some examples of minor violations:

   - Excessive tardiness;
   - Unsatisfactory job performance;
   - Defacing company property;
   - Interfering with another employee's job performance;
   - Excessive absenteeism;
   - Failure to observe working hours, such as the schedule of starting time, quitting time, rest and meal periods;
   - Performing unauthorized personal work on company time;
   - Failure to notify the vice president of intended absence either before or within one hour after the start of a shift;
   - Unauthorized use of the company telephone or equipment for personal business.

2. Major Violations — These more serious violations would include any deliberate or willful infraction of company rules and may preclude continued employment of an employee. Here are some examples of major violations:

   - Fighting on company premises;
   - Repeated occurrences of related or unrelated minor violations, depending upon the severity of the violation and the circumstances;
   - Any act which might endanger the safety or lives of others;
   - Departing company premises during working hours for personal reasons without the permission of the vice president;
   - Bringing firearms or weapons onto the company premises;
   - Deliberately stealing, destroying, abusing, or damaging company property, tools, or equipment, or the property of another employee or visitor;

▶

Performance Improvement — continued 290.1

- Disclosure of confidential company information or trade secrets to unauthorized persons;
- Willfully disregarding company policies or procedures;
- Willfully falsifying any company records; or
- Failing to report to work without excuse or approval of management for three consecutive days.

Terminations 295

Comment: Terminations are very costly to an organization in the following ways:

- Employee Turnover — The company's investment in training the employee and grooming him or her to be a valuable and active part of the company work force is lost.
- Corrective Counseling — The amount of rehabilitation time invested by management in assisting the employee in a performance improvement program is, to some extent, wasted.
- Dismissal — The amount of time spent by management to define appropriate action for employee discipline is nonproductive.
- Layoff — Company morale and productivity are reduced as everyone becomes anxious that they may be the next to receive a layoff notice.

Terminations, however, are inevitable within any organization. You should develop clearly stated procedures that are flexible enough to handle the various forms of termination.

In deciding on the policies and procedures for terminations, you should be aware of certain legal traps. Discussion of these traps in conjunction with this policy does not mean that you should include an exhaustive list of do's and don'ts into an already lengthy policy. But failing to recognize these traps could certainly affect your company's profits just because of the legal fees incurred for defending a lawsuit or administrative proceeding, not to mention the potential for court judgments or fines against the company or its officers. An employer should consult with an expert both at the time of writing this policy and if a termination appears to involve some potential for legal entanglement. You should consider a seminar, led by an authoritative professional, for you and your management team on these issues. Although our intent is to be informative, the following comments are not to be considered as a complete discussion of all the legal issues related to terminations.

Many states have statutes which require that final wages be paid to a terminated employee on the final day of work. Some make the failure to pay final wages a crime or subject to a penalty.[1] Some states also have statutes governing the payment of final wages to an employee who voluntarily terminates. For instance, the time of payment may depend upon the amount of notice given by the employee. States may also have statutes requiring special treatment for employees in special occupations who are laid off.[2]

In most cases, state law requires that pay for vested vacation time and vested sick leave be included in the final paycheck. Some statutes specifically prohibit the forfeiture of vested vacation pay upon termination whether or not for cause.[3] "Vested" generally means that the time off is permanently credited to the employee and is readily available or convertible to money. Local statutory and case law should be consulted, especially regarding the issue of when vacation pay vests. In some states, notably California, vacation pay has been held to vest as the services are performed and is equivalent to wages.[4]

Another issue is raised when the employee owes the company money (e.g., for a travel expense advance) and is terminated before repayment. Can the employer legally deduct this money from the final paycheck? Although most employers would be surprised to learn otherwise, most states prohibit this practice unless the employee has signed a written consent to this practice before the money is advanced to the employee. Obviously, state laws will differ on this issue.

Employers should also be advised to consult state and federal law regarding anti-retaliation laws. Generally, an employer is prohibited from disciplining or discharging an employee just because he or she filed a discrimination claim, a labor grievance, or a workers' compensation claim, to name a few protected activities. Many laws make such retaliation a crime and impose fines or imprisonment or both for violations. Carefully review your state's list of unlawful employment practices as you prepare your policy manual. Also, the National Labor Relations Act[5] (NLRA) protects employees from discrimination — discharge or other disciplinary reprisals — for engaging in protected "concerted activity." This phrase "concerted activity" generally includes the exercise of the employee's statutory rights under the NLRA; however, an activity that is concerned with the terms or conditions of employment and is of mutual concern to a group of employees, probably two or more, will be protected. Protection is granted regardless of whether or not there is a collective bargaining agreement in existence. The situation is generally not as one-sided as it may first seem. For instance, an employer can discipline or discharge an employee who engages in an unprotected strike or work stoppage.

Special consideration must be given to the termination of an employee for theft, fraud, or other crimes committed on company premises. In such cases, the use of suspension, which is a provision of Performance Improvement, Section 2150, should be considered for the following reasons:

- The need to make a more thorough investigation is warranted;
- Other employees, especially informers, may need some protection;
- Company property may be vandalized or removed in retaliation.

Although the authors recommend that all terminations be handled in a confidential manner, this is especially so when the cause of termination is crime-related.

The best approach is to reveal the circumstances of the termination to only those staff members who must know. Otherwise, the terminated employee may sue you and the company for defamation or invasion of privacy. A recent case in California held that public posting of an employee's termination established a *prima facie* case of invasion of privacy under the California Constitution.[6] If you use the threat of reporting the matter to the police as leverage for the employee's resignation, you may be charged with extortion.

By now you have read the **Comment** to the Performance Improvement policy which precedes this discussion. The erosion of the employer's right to discharge an employee at will has been occurring in California and other states for some time. This is occurring in California despite a state statute which clearly sets forth the "employment at will" doctrine.[7] Other states probably have similar laws.

Several legal concepts have emerged to hold employers liable for wrongful discharge of an employee. Listed below are some of these legal concepts.

- Public policy — The employee was told to do an illegal act, refused, and was fired.[8]
- Intentional infliction of emotional distress — Conduct by an employer considered to be outrageous could result in liability to the employer.[9]
- Retaliatory discharge — The employee was terminated after signing a union membership application.[10]
- Breach of written contract — A contract that provided for permanent employment as long as the employee operated in a competent, profitable, and efficient manner.[11]
- Bad faith, malice, or ill will — The employee was discharged for refusing to date the foreman.[12]
- Exercising a statutory right — The employee was discharged for filing a workers' compensation claim.[13]
- Breach of oral contract — This claim was based on a promise of permanent employment, as long as employee's work is satisfactory, and further oral assurances made by the company that termination would occur only for good cause.[14]
- Breach of implied covenant of good faith and fair dealing in an oral contract — An employee with 18 years seniority was terminated, and the company failed to follow its grievance procedure.[15]
- Implied agreement to discharge for only good cause — It was found upon the termination of a corporate officer, who had been employed for 32 years and received commendations and promotions without derogatory performance appraisals, was given assurances of continued employment.[16]
- Breach of contract — The employee policies and handbook, when considered together, were evidence of "good cause only" discharge policy. The court held that these company communications became part of the employment contract which was admittedly oral.[17]

There are other cases, too numerous to mention, from other states. Anytime an employee takes action which he or she is legally entitled to take, such as filing statutory claims for benefits or making a charge of discriminatory practices, the employee is protected from discharge or discipline for doing so. There are many federal and state statutes providing such protection. If the employee is subsequently discharged or disciplined for some misconduct warranting it, be prepared to present documentary evidence to support the independent reason for the discharge or discipline.

Your company policies and procedures, when read together, should not be susceptible to the interpretation that permanent or long-term employment is promised. The authors have endeavored to avoid this interpretation in these policies and procedures, but no one can predict how a judge or jury will interpret a particular set of facts. If possible, your employment application and your policies should conspicuously state the employment-at-will doctrine.

If you adopt an appeal procedure, make sure it is followed. At a minimum, any appeal procedure should provide the employee with a right to know the charges or alleged misconduct, to hear the evidence against him or her, to present documentary and oral evidence on his or her behalf before a neutral decision maker, and to have a sufficient time to prepare for this hearing.

If a corrective counseling policy is adopted, follow it, and ensure that the process is documented. If your termination policy provides examples of misconduct, which will lead to discipline or immediate discharge, do not try to make the list all-inclusive. State that the examples of misconduct are not limited to those listed. Above all, you must treat all employees fairly and evenhandedly and apply your written policies consistently.

You should examine all company communications and any other personnel or benefit-related documents for the flaws cited above. You should also adopt a mandatory policy of no promises of long term or permanent employment by anyone to anyone. Even use of the words "career opportunity" in employment ads or personnel requisitions is suspect. Lastly, avoid the words "fair cause," "good cause" or any such implications that can defeat the employment-at-will doctrine.

Remember also that the words and actions of supervisory personnel can give rise to unintended rights or benefits in favor of employees. Make certain that supervisory personnel understand the policy manual and act in a manner consistent with it.

Now the other side of the coin. Some employers believe that taking all of the above steps, especially emphasizing the right to discharge at will in various documents, may damage employee morale or cause good prospective employees to go elsewhere. Frankly, this may be the case, unless you diplomatically word your company communications to set a softer tone. If you feel this way, then adopt policies which reflect your own style of management. If you desire some type of appeal or grievance procedure, draft one that is fair to both sides. You may not prevent a wrongful discharge lawsuit from being brought, but you can at least show that the termination process was fair and that the employee was afforded those rights and still lost.

Several common themes appear in these cases. First, a representation of some kind was made by someone with apparent supervisory authority. Representations include statements in a policy manual, verbal promises or assurances, or past conduct of an employer in response to similar situations. As noted, what you do is as important as what you say. Make certain that your managers understand the policy manual and act consistently with it. Second, don't discharge an employee for exercising a statutory right. Third, don't engage in conduct which by all objective standards is outrageous or would tend to shock the conscience of a judge or jury.

We cannot overemphasize enough that the disciplinary or termination process must be confidential. When you terminate someone, do so privately. In detail, explain exactly why the person is being terminated, using your documentation as backup. Explain the appeal or grievance process to the employee, and let the employee exercise those rights. You can be polite, but be firm; stick to your carefully thought-out policy.

Two policies regarding terminations are provided on the following pages. The right to discharge at will is included in the second policy. The first policy could be interpreted to mean that the employer can only discharge "for cause" (e.g., substandard performance, misconduct) or layoff. No appeal or grievance procedure is provided in either policy. It is probably better to consult someone familiar with local law before finalizing such a procedure.

If you desire to use the second policy and reserve your at will rights, make sure that any corrective counseling or performance improvement policy also contains the same appropriate language or is tailored to achieve this result.

Because terminations are costly, many companies are evaluating each employee termination through an exit interview. The interviews may be a source of vital information that can eventually reduce employee turnover and increase productivity and profit. A sample Exit Interview Guide follows the policies presented in this discussion.

Without question, case law and statutory law, which impact terminations and the related issue of plant closings, continue to evolve. Consult with your legal counsel as you prepare your policy manual and periodically thereafter, so that your manual will stay current with any changes in law.

Terminations Alternate Policy 1 295.1

Terminations are to be treated in a confidential, professional manner by all concerned. The (COMPANY) must assure thorough, consistent, and evenhanded termination procedures. This policy and its administration will be implemented in accordance with the company equal opportunity statement.

Note: *You may choose to include the preceding sentence in a separate guide for supervisory personnel and eliminate it from the policy manual.*

Terminating employees are entitled to receive all earned pay, including vacation pay.

Note: *If you do not have a "vested" vacation policy you will want to delete or modify the preceding sentence in accordance with local law.*

Only employees with 15 or more years of service with the company, as explained in the policy, Sick or Personal Leave, Section 420, are qualified to receive sick or personal leave payout.

Note: *Again the preceding sentence must be consistent with your sick or personal leave policy and local law.*

Employment with the company is normally terminated through one of the following actions:

1. Resignation — voluntary termination by the employee;

2. Dismissal — involuntary termination for substandard performance or misconduct;

3. Layoff — termination due to reduction of the workforce or elimination of a position.

▶

Terminations — continued Alternate Policy 1 295.1

Resignation

An employee desiring to terminate employment, regardless of employee classification, is expected to give as much advance notice as possible. Two weeks or 10 working days is generally considered to be sufficient notice time.

Should an employee resign to join a competitor, if there is any other conflict of interest, or if the employee refuses to reveal the circumstances of his or her resignation and the future employer, the manager may require the employee to leave the company immediately rather than work during the notice period. This is not to be construed as a reflection upon the employee's integrity but an action in the best interests of business practice. When immediate voluntary termination occurs for the above reasons, the employee will receive pay "in lieu of notice," the maximum being two weeks of pay based upon a 40-hour workweek at the employee's straight-time rate or salary.

Dismissal

1. Substandard Performance — An employee may be discharged if his or her performance is unacceptable. The vice president shall have counseled the employee concerning performance deficiencies, provided direction for improvement, and warned the employee of possible termination if performance did not improve within a defined period of time. The vice president is expected to be alert to any underlying reasons for performance deficiencies such as personal problems or substance abuse. Documentation to be prepared by the vice president shall include reason for separation, performance history, corrective efforts taken, alternatives explored, and any additional pertinent information.

▶

Terminations — continued Alternate Policy 1 295.1

2. Misconduct — An employee found to be engaged in activities such as, but not limited to, theft of company property, insubordination, conflict of interest, or any other activities showing willful disregard of company interests or policies, will be terminated.

   Note: *See Performance Improvement, Section 290, for a list of other examples.*

   Termination resulting from misconduct shall be entered into the employee's personnel file. The employee shall be provided with a written summary of the reason for termination. No salary continuance or severance pay will be allowed.

Layoff

When a reduction in force is necessary or if one or more positions are eliminated, employees will be identified for layoff after evaluating the following factors:

1. Company work requirements;
2. Employee's abilities, experience, and skill;
3. Employee's potential for reassignment within the organization; and
4. Length of service.

Note: *No priority is intended, but your policy can be modified to specify a priority.*

The immediate vice president will personally notify employees of a layoff. After explaining the layoff procedure, the employee will be given a letter describing the conditions of the layoff, such as the effect the layoff will have on his or her anniversary date at time of call-back; the procedure to be followed if time off to seek other employment is granted; and the

▶

Terminations — continued Alternate Policy 1 295.1

company's role in assisting employees to find other work. The employee and the vice president will follow one of the following procedures:

1. The employee will receive at least two weeks advance notice of termination date.
2. The employee will be terminated immediately and will receive one week of pay for each year of employment with the company in lieu of notice, up to a maximum of four weeks. The payment will be based on a 40-hour workweek at the employee's straight time rate or salary.

Note: *Your policy may be silent on such a determination which leaves it up to management to decide, but the determination must be made evenhandedly.*

Termination Processing Procedures

1. Upon any termination,a termination checklist must be initiated. The (VICE PRESIDENT) will direct and coordinate the termination procedure.
2. All outstanding advances charged to the terminating employee will be deducted from the final paycheck.

   Note: *Some states limit this procedure in the absence of a signed written agreement entered into prior to the advance, so check local law.*
3. On the final day of employment, the (VICE PRESIDENT) must receive all keys, ID cards, and company property from the employee.
4. The (VICE PRESIDENT) shall conduct an exit interview with the employee.

   Note: *A sample Exit Interview Guide is provided at the end of this section.*
5. The employee will pick up his or her final payroll check at the time of the exit interview. The final check shall include all earned pay and any expenses due the employee.

Terminations Alternate Policy 2 295.2

Terminations are to be treated in a confidential, professional manner by all concerned. The company must assure thorough, consistent, and evenhanded termination procedures. This policy and its administration will be implemented in accordance with the company equal opportunity statement.

Note: *You may choose to include the preceding sentence in a separate guide for supervisory personnel and eliminate it from the policy manual.*

Inasmuch as an employee can terminate his or her employment with the company at any time and for any reason, (COMPANY) can terminate an employee at any time and for any reason with or without cause. The company subscribes to the policy of employment at will. Continued employment with the company is at the sole and exclusive option of company management. Permanent employment or employment for a specific term cannot be guaranteed or promised.

Note: *It is recommended that the two preceding sentences be inserted in a conspicuous place at the beginning of the company employment application.*

In the absence of a specific written contract of employment between an employee and the company no promises or guarantees of permanent or specific term employment will be made to an employee by anyone, nor will such promises or guarantees, if made, ever be adhered to by the company or enforced by the employee.

Terminating employees are entitled to receive all earned pay, including vacation pay.

Note: *If you do not have a "vested" vacation policy, you will want to delete or modify the preceding sentence in accordance with local law.*

▶

Terminations — continued Alternate Policy 2 295.2

Unused sick or personal time will be forfeited.

Note: *Again check your sick or personal leave policy and local law.*

Employment with the company is normally terminated through one of the following actions:

1. Resignation — voluntary termination by the employee;
2. Dismissal — involuntary termination by the company for any reason at any time with or without cause;
3. Layoff — termination due to reduction of the work force or elimination of a position.

Resignation

An employee desiring to terminate employment, regardless of employee classification, is expected to give as much notice as possible. Two weeks or 10 working days is generally considered to be sufficient notice time to find a replacement.

Should an employee resign to join a competitor, if there is any other conflict of interest, or if the employee refuses to reveal the circumstances of his or her resignation and the future employer, the vice president may require the employee to leave the company immediately rather than work during the notice period. This is not to be construed as a reflection upon the employee's integrity but an action in the best interests of business practice. When immediate voluntary termination occurs for the above reasons, the employee will receive pay "in lieu of notice," the maximum being two weeks of pay based upon a 40-hour work-week at the employee's straight-time rate or salary.

▶

Terminations — continued Alternate Policy 2 295.2

Employees terminating voluntarily are entitled to receive all earned vacation pay.

Note: *If you do not have a "vested" vacation policy, you will want to delete or modify the preceding sentence in accordance with local law.*

Unused sick or personal time will be forfeited.

Note: *Again, check your sick or personal leave policy and local law.*

Dismissal

An employee may be dismissed at any time, for any reason, with or without cause, at the sole and absolute discretion of company management. In the case of dismissal, the company may, in its sole discretion, give some notice of its intent to dismiss an employee, but the company is not required to give any such notice.

Layoff

When a reduction in force is necessary, or one or more positions are eliminated, the company will, in its sole discretion, identify the employees to be laid off. The company may give two weeks notice to the laid off employee, but it reserves the right to substitute two weeks severance pay in lieu of notice. Such pay will be based upon a 40-hour workweek at the employee's straight-time rate or salary.

Termination Processing Procedures

1. Upon any termination, a termination checklist must be initiated. The (VICE PRESIDENT) will direct and coordinate the termination procedure.

▶

Terminations — continued Alternate Policy 2 295.2

2. All outstanding advances charged to the terminating employee will be deducted from the final paycheck.

   Note: *Some states limit this procedure in the absence of a signed written agreement entered into prior to the advance, so check local law.*

3. On the final day of employment, the (VICE PRESIDENT) must receive all keys, ID cards, and company property from the employee.
4. The (VICE PRESIDENT) shall conduct an exit interview with the employee.

Note: *A sample Exit Interview Guide is provided at the end of this section.*

5. The employee will pick up his or her final payroll check at the time of the exit interview. The final check shall include all earned pay and any expenses due the employee.

EXIT INTERVIEW GUIDE

Note: *An exit interview, properly conducted, can give an employer information about the climate within the company; company morale; and the attitude of employees toward their supervisors, management, and their fellow employees. It is important to build rapport by asking non-threatening questions similar to the following:*

1. Which responsibilities did you like most about the job? Which responsibilities did you like the least?
2. What did you like most about the department you were assigned to?
3. What did you think about the way the manager handled complaints?
4. What type of working conditions are most conducive to your best productivity?
5. What do you see as the future of this company?
6. What impressed you about this company when you first accepted your position? Has this impression changed? If so, how? Why?
7. When you first joined the company, was your training helpful for what you were actually doing six months later?
8. What type of job are you going to? What are you looking for in that position that you feel is not present in this company?
9. What kind of work do you like to do best? Were you doing that kind of work in your job here?
10. What points would you want to make if you could tell top management how you felt about this organization?
11. How do you feel about the contribution you have made to this company?
12. Tell me what your feelings are about the benefit program offered by this company?

Note: *In analyzing the responses, watch for patterns that may provide helpful information for the employee selection process. The responses may also provide suggestions for improvement in the general organizational or personnel areas.*

Footnotes

200 — Equal Opportunity

1. 42 U.S.C. (United States Code) § 2000e-2000e-17.
2. 42 U.S.C. § 1981.
3. 29 U.S.C. § 206.
4. 29 U.S.C. § 201–219.
5. 29 U.S.C. § 621–634.

295 — Terminations

1. Cal. Lab. Code § 201, 203.
2. Cal. Lab. Code § 201, 201.5, 201.7.
3. Cal. Lab. Code § 227.3.
4. Saustez v. Plastic Dress-up Co., 31 Cal.3d 774, 183 Cal. Rptr. 846 (1982).
5. 29 U.S.C. § 158(a)(1).
6. Payton v. City of Santa Clara, 132 Cal. App.3d 152, 183 Cal. Rptr. 17 (1982).
7. Cal. Lab. Code § 2922.
8. Tameny v. Atlantic Richfield Co., 27 Cal.3d 167, 164 Cal. Rptr. 839 (1980).
9. Agis v. Howard Johnson Company, 371 Mass. 140, 355 N.E.2d 315 (1976).
10. Glenn v. Clearman's Golden Cock Inn, Inc., 192 Cal. App.2d 793, 13 Cal. Rptr. 769 (1961).
11. Drzewiecki v. H & R Block, Inc., 24 Cal. App.3d 695, 101 Cal. Rptr. 169 (1972).
12. Monge v. Beebe Rubber Co., 316 A.2d 549 (N.H. 1974).
13. Frampton v. Central Indiana Gas Co., 297 N.E.2d 425 (Ind. 1973).
14. Rabago-Alvarez v. Dart Industries, Inc., 55 Cal. App.3d 91, 127 Cal. Rptr. 222 (1976).
15. Cleary v. American Airlines, Inc., 111 Cal. App.3d 443, 168 Cal. Rptr. 722 (1980).
16. Pugh v. See's Candies, Inc., 116 Cal. App.3d 311, 171 Cal. Rptr. 917 (1981).
17. Toussaint v. Blue Cross of Michigan, 408 Mich. 579, 292 N.W.2d 880 (1980).

Chapter 3
Compensation

Introduction

The monetary rewards that your employees receive in exchange for their intellectual, emotional, and physical efforts have a significant effect on your company's success. Although the nonmonetary factors of a job contribute greatly to employees' job satisfaction and productivity, the effect of compensation cannot be ignored.

The challenge in the development of the policies for this section of your policy manual is to provide a fair and equitable compensation package that enables you to provide quality products or services at competitive prices and stimulates your employees to exert that effort which results in quality production. The policies discussed in this chapter permit your company to attract and maintain outstanding employees. On the other hand, your compensation package must ensure a profit for your company.

Compensation is also a source of conflict, especially where employees within the same classification compare and contrast what their fellow employees are being paid. As a result, the confidential nature of compensation should be stressed.

Equal Pay 300

Comment: As noted earlier in Section 200, Equal Opportunity, federal and state statutes require equal pay or comparable worth for men and women performing similar services. Failure to do so can result in a claim based on wage or sex discrimination. A general policy statement concerning equal pay follows.

Equal Pay 300.1

(COMPANY) will not pay wages to any employee at a rate less than the company pays employees of the opposite sex for comparable work requiring comparable skills. This policy is to be construed in accordance with applicable federal and state laws and regulations.

Position Descriptions 310

Comment: A well-defined description for each position within your company is a valuable asset. Taken as a whole, position descriptions are similar to a blueprint: they define the parts of a company's organization and detail every part's specifications. The specifications include job qualifications, assigned duties, responsibilities, knowledge, coordination, reporting requirements, and physical working conditions. Management's analysis and review of all the company position descriptions may also uncover overlapping duties. It will also identify employee responsibilities that might be more effectively assigned to another position.

A good position description should define the job to be accomplished. It helps the employee understand what the job entails and what the company expects of him or her. A position description encourages high employee productivity and is a tool which provides the standards to measure an employee's performance. This is especially true when the employee is involved in creating the position description, as suggested in Alternate Policy 1 on the following page.

A complete set of position descriptions will assist management in structuring or restructuring the company organization. They are also a basis for determining employee classifications and compensation levels. As such, they assist your company to comply with various federal laws, such as the Fair Labor Standards Act, the Equal Pay Act, and Title VII, because they contain essential information which helps determine the following:

- Exempt and nonexempt classifications;
- Equal pay for equal work; and
- The existence of artificial employment barriers.

All of your position descriptions should be in the same format. Personnel responsible for developing them should receive similar training and follow the same guidelines. The position descriptions should provide a balanced and integrated picture of your organization and each one should be reviewed periodically and updated when necessary. This will ensure that they accurately describe each employee's responsibilities and his or her relationship to others within the organization.

For your convenience, a sample Position Description Form follows Alternate Policy 2.

Position Descriptions Alternate Policy 1 310.1

The purpose of position descriptions at (COMPANY) is to define a position's duties and set requirements for filling the position. Within three months after every employee has filled a position, a personalized position description detailing the unique features of the job and establishing the employee's job objectives will be prepared by each supervisor using input from the employee. The previous position description will be used as a model in defining the present employee's position. A supervisor shall review an employee's position description when he or she requests it.

All position descriptions shall include the following information:

1. Title of position;
2. Assigned organizational unit (e.g., payroll, marketing);
3. Position classification number;
4. Position summary or overview;
5. Position qualifications (minimum qualifications including job experience, skills, and education); and
6. Major duties and responsibilities.

These position descriptions are used to compare our positions with the positions of other companies for salary surveys. Position descriptions are also one of the factors used in setting the pay scale of positions within our company. Management shall review all position descriptions annually to ensure equity and consistency within and across job families and functional lines.

Position Descriptions Alternate Policy 2 310.2

Position descriptions are available for all positions in the company. The items included in each position description are the following:

1. Job identification;
2. Job qualifications;
3. Summary statement;
4. Assigned responsibilities or duties; and
5. Supervisor or rater.

Position descriptions are used to determine employee selection, job requirements, performance appraisals, organizational structure, and the relative worth of jobs in relation to each other. Company management annually reviews all company positions to ensure equity and consistency in our human resource system.

POSITION DESCRIPTION

Job Title: ________________________ Job Code: ____________

Department: ________________________ Date: ____________

Written By: ________________________

Approved By: ________________________

Pay Scale: ______________ Exempt ________ Nonexempt ________

Qualifications: ________________________

____

____

____

____

____

____

Summary Statement: ________________________

____

____

____

____

____

____

____

____

____

____

____

Assigned Responsibilities or Duties: ________________________

____

____

____

____

____

____

Supervisor: ________________________

Workday, Payday, and Pay Advances 320–40

Comment: Time worked is defined by the Fair Labor Standards Act (FLSA) and by the laws or regulations of most states. Under federal law, work not requested but "suffered or permitted" is compensable. That means that if an employer knows or has reason to believe that an employee is working, the employer must pay for the time worked. Having a rule or policy that no overtime will be permitted is not sufficient. The employer must also make certain that the policy is being enforced.

Meal periods are compensable time unless the employee is completely relieved from his or her work. Rest periods are compensable time regardless. See the **Comment** to Meal and Rest Periods, Section 360.

Preparatory or concluding activities are compensable if they are an integral part of the employee's principal activity — cleaning up around a machine before leaving. However, preparatory or concluding activities are not compensable if they are allowed for the employee's convenience only, e.g., washing up. Likewise, travel to and from work is not compensable time; however, an employment agreement or a collective bargaining contract can vary the rules regarding travel and preparatory and concluding activities.

A discussion of who is or is not covered by the Fair Labor Standards Act is contained in the **Comment** to Overtime Compensation, Section 350. Most states have laws regarding what is or is not time worked, and typically, they will parallel the FLSA.

Your policy should define what hours will be considered as the company workday, for example, 8:00 A.M. to 5:00 P.M. If your company has two or more shifts, it would be appropriate to define them as well, either in this policy or in a separate policy on shifts. Also, you should define your company pay periods.

Frequency of paydays is regulated by state law for most employers. One exception is under the Davis–Bacon Act which applies to employers who hire mechanics and laborers working on federal building construction contracts, including alterations and painting. Under that law, employers must pay weekly.

Typically, state laws or regulations will require an employer to pay all employees at a specified frequency — weekly, biweekly, or monthly. Exceptions to the general rule may also be provided for certain employee classifications, e.g., executive or management employees may only have to be paid once a month instead of twice a month. Obviously, you can pay more frequently than the law requires; however, there is usually a specific law or regulation pertaining to terminated employees.

State legislation will also set limitations on how long you can postpone payment for work performed earlier. For example, in California, work that is performed between the 1st and 15th of the month must be compensated between the 16th and 26th of the same month; work performed between the 16th and the end of the month must be compensated between the 1st and 10th of the following month.[1] You will usually be required to post a notice of the company paydays and the time and place of payment in a conspicuous place on the premises.[2]

For every employee, it is vital that you maintain complete and accurate records of all hours worked daily and weekly, pay rates, time off with and without pay, time of day and day of workweek that begins and ends, total daily or weekly straight-time earnings, overtime compensation, additions to or deductions from gross earnings for each pay period, total wages paid each pay period, dates of those payments, and the inclusive dates of each pay period.[3] You should also have a record of every employee's name, Social Security number, address, sex, and occupation. Every employee must receive an itemized statement of gross wages, all deductions, net wages, inclusive dates of the pay period, employee's name or Social Security number, and the employer's name and address for every pay period.

The majority of companies pay on a biweekly basis with time cards or time sheets being submitted to the payroll department three to five days prior to payday. Typically, employees are responsible for recording and reporting their hours worked.

The sample Time Sheet located after the alternate policies on workdays requests the very basic information of time-in for the morning, time-out at noon, time back after lunch, and time-out at the end of the day. Columns are provided for calculating regular and overtime hours. Dates and times are recorded on a semimonthly period. The employee's and supervisor's signatures certify the hours worked and approved. The check number provides an audit trail for the accounting department. A legend might be added at the bottom of the time sheet, designating "R"–regular, "S"–sick, "H"–Holiday, "V"–Vacation; and these letters can be used in identifying hours for each pay period.

Advances in pay may be authorized by this policy, if it is your desire to make this benefit available to your employees. Some companies prohibit it. Other companies allow for it in emergency situations only. Rarely do companies provide this benefit without any limitations. Collecting and accounting for a pay advance can be a headache for your payroll department and a burden on an employee. Abuses are hard to prevent, and errors can be demoralizing.

If you grant an advance pay benefit, be sure that you have a previous written, signed, and dated authorization from the employee to justify the later deduction. It should also authorize you to deduct the full remaining balance from the employee's last paycheck. It would be best to inform the employee, on the authorization itself, how much will be deducted from his or her future paychecks. If the employee terminates or doesn't come back to work, you are probably stuck if his or her last paycheck is insufficient to cover what is owed. If you prohibit pay advances, you may still want to consider vacation pay advances which involve less risk. A sample Payroll Advance Request Form follows Alternate Policy 1 on Payroll Advances.

For your convenience, the issues discussed above have been segregated into separate policies to enable you to pick and choose policies for your manual. With only minor modifications, these policies can be combined to form one policy.

Workday Alternate Policy 1 320.1

A workday begins at (ADD START TIME) and ends at (ADD FINISH TIME) with (ADD NUMBER) hour off for lunch. Each workweek consists of (ADD NUMBER) hours, and generally includes work performed Monday through Friday. However, the nature of our business sometimes demands workday or workweek hours different than those set forth above. Variation to the schedule will be made or approved by (VICE PRESIDENT).

Workday Alternate Policy 2 320.2

Specific workday and workweek hours for each employee will be determined from time to time based on the operational needs of the company. (COMPANY) will attempt to notify employees of any changes in workdays or workweek hours two weeks in advance of the effective date of any such change.

TIME SHEET

Name: ______________________________ Week(s) ending: ________ 19____

Date	Time in	Time out	Time in	Time out	Regular Hours	Overtime Hours

TOTAL HOURS (Regular and Overtime): ______________

Employee's Signature: ____

Supervisor's Signature: ____

Check #: _______________

Payday Alternate Policy 1 330.1

Our employees are paid every two weeks, 26 times annually. The first payday of the year will be on the first (DAY) of the month, with each successive payday being on alternate (DAY). Time cards are to be submitted by close of business the Friday preceding the company payday. Pay is for the two workweeks preceding the next payday.

Payday Alternate Policy 2 330.2

The company paydays are the 5th and 20th of each month. Employees are to submit their time card or time sheet three working days prior to the 5th and 20th of the month. For paydays that fall during the weekend, checks will be distributed on the Friday prior to the payday. If a company holiday falls on the 5th or 20th, employees will receive their payroll check on the last workday prior to the holiday.

Pay Advances Alternate Policy 1 340.1

An employee pay advance is a temporary cash advance of an amount no more than (ADD DOLLAR AMOUNT), repayable in (ADD NUMBER) pay periods. The pay advance is interest free and is granted only in the event of an employee emergency. The determination to grant or reject an advance request is made in the sole discretion of (COMPANY). The advance is obtained by filling out a payroll advance request and submitting it through the vice president for processing. Requests for additional advances will be processed only after the initial advance is repaid.

Note: *A Payroll Advance Request Form is included on the following page.*

All arrangements for mailing or depositing employee paychecks must be made in advance and in writing.

PAYROLL ADVANCE REQUEST

Employee Name: ____

Date of Advance: ____________________ Request Advance Amount: $ ______________

Agreement:

I, the undersigned employee, in consideration of the above advance pay given to me by (COMPANY), hereby irrevocably authorize the (COMPANY) Payroll Department to deduct the above advance amount in equal installments from the net earnings payable to me for the (ADD NUMBER) pay period(s) immediately following the date of receipt of the advance amount. I understand that each such deduction shall be (ADD DOLLAR AMOUNT). I fully understand and agree that the total of all payroll deductions for repayment of this advance shall be equal to the total amount advanced in accordance with the above schedule.

I further understand and agree that my acceptance of the advance amount and this related authorization for payroll deduction shall in no way be construed as a contract for my continued employment with (COMPANY). In the event of my termination of employment with (COMPANY), whether voluntary or involuntary, prior to the total recovery by (COMPANY) of the amount advanced to me, I authorize (COMPANY) to deduct the full remaining balance of this advance from my final paycheck. In the event my final paycheck is insufficient to repay the advance, I recognize my absolute and irrevocable obligation to fully repay any remaining balance to (COMPANY) after my final paycheck has been credited against the advance amount owed and to pay reasonable attorneys fees incurred by (COMPANY) in the event collection efforts are required.

Signatures:

____ ________________

Employee Date

Approved by:

____ ________________

Vice President Date

Pay Advances Alternate Policy 2 340.2

It is our policy to decline all requests for early paychecks or pay advances for personal reasons. Pay advances in the event of vacation or legitimate business reasons (e.g., temporary duty assignment) may be requested through the vice president.

Overtime Compensation 350

Comment: In establishing a company policy for overtime compensation, consideration must be given to federal and state legislation and regulations governing wage and salary practices. Some of the legislation is generally reviewed below; however, prior to establishing a company policy in this area, it is important to seek expert assistance from federal or state, or both, agencies or an attorney to ensure compliance with all applicable laws.

The Fair Labor Standards Act of 1938 (FLSA) covers four areas: minimum wage, equal pay, overtime, and child labor standards. These comments only pertain to the general rules regarding overtime compensation and typical exemptions from those provisions.

Generally, the FLSA applies to the employer–employee relationship and not to the employer–independent contractor relationship. The primary factor in determining the employment relationship is the amount of control the employer has over the employee, but the test is liberally construed in favor of finding the employer–employee relationship. An employer who incorrectly characterizes a relationship as an independent contractual one can incur significant liability, including personal liability, for Social Security and federal and state unemployment taxes which were not withheld. Other tests may be used, and consultation with your attorney is recommended.

If the employee–employer relationship exists and if either the employee or the employer is subject to the FLSA, compliance is required. In order to be subject to the FLSA, either the employee or the employer must be engaged in interstate commerce. If the employee is so engaged, then only he or she is covered by the FLSA. If the employer is covered, then all of the employees are covered whether they individually are engaged in interstate commerce or not.

Some businesses are specifically named in the Act as being covered, e.g., clothing or fabric laundering, cleaning, or repairing. You should seek expert advice if you are in doubt about whether the FLSA applies to your company or your employees.

The Act requires that all employees who work in excess of a 40-hour workweek must be paid at a rate of one and one-half times their "regular rate" for all hours worked in excess of 40. "Regular rate" is defined in the Act. Each workweek stands alone and hours may not be averaged over two or more workweeks. Once an employee's workweek has been established, it may be changed but only if the change is not designed to avoid paying overtime.

The FLSA defines a number of distinct employee classification exemptions, even if those employees are engaged in interstate commerce or the employer is covered. The more commonly used exemptions are: executive, administrative, professional, and outside sales. Remember, the Act specifies more than these four, and it would be wise to check if one of these covers some or all of your employees. The Act and its accompanying regulations provide certain tests and examples to assist employers in determining whether or not particular employees are exempt. The regulations are complex and not capable of brief description. Employers would be well served to review the regulations or consult their legal advisers.

Generally, if an executive, administrative, or professional employee performs certain enumerated duties and responsibilities and is paid a salary of $250 per week or more, the employee is exempt from mandatory overtime compensation. However, certain employees paid a salary of less than $250 per week, but at least $155 per week, who meet the additional duties and responsibilities required by the regulations, will also be exempt.

The exemption for outside salespeople is detailed in a series of federal regulations. Generally, a salesperson must be employed to make sales or take orders, not to provide service. He or she must be customarily and regularly doing such sales work away from the employer's place of business. Additionally, work other than that described above, or incidental to it, such as writing sales reports or attending sales meeting, must not exceed 20% of the workweek hours of nonexempt employees. The outside salesperson is exempt if he or she meets these requirements.

The burden of proof falls on the employer claiming an exemption. The authors emphasize the need to use caution and to consult an expert in this area for specific advice relating to coverage and exemptions. We do not recommend that you try to delineate the definition of exempt and nonexempt classifications in your policy without expert assistance, unless you do so in the most general of terms. See the policy, Employee Classifications, Section 240.

Other federal laws besides the FLSA also regulate wages and hours. These laws, however, apply only if you have a federal government contract or subcontract, and only if the value of the contract exceeds a specified limit — usually very low. They include The Walsh–Healy Act ("goods," $10,000+); The Davis–Bacon Act (construction of public buildings or alterations, $2,000+); The Contract Work Hours Standards Act (again, construction; expands the FLSA coverage for overtime to all hours in excess of eight in one day in addition to those in excess of 40 in one week); and The Service Contract Act (services, $2,500). Generally, the terms, conditions, and requirements of the applicable laws will be referred to in the documents which solicit bids or proposals for the particular contracts or in the contracts themselves.

Caution: A warning is appropriate for the unwary. All of these laws carry penalties to encourage compliance. Civil suits by the employee or the government are specified. Certain willful violations are crimes and may result in heavy fines or imprisonment of officers and directors. Officers and directors may have personal liability for unpaid amounts as well; and if you violate the laws that apply to federal government contractors, you may have these fines or judgments withheld from future contract payments, and you may be barred from future contracts for a specific period of time.

Naturally, you also will have to comply with state laws and regulations in this area, and all states have legislation on wages and hours. You may find, for instance, that your state requires all employers to pay overtime to employees who work in excess of 8 hours in any given day as well as for the hours worked over the 40-hour standard workweek. Some states, such as California, require double time for all hours over 12 in one day or on holidays. Sometimes the exemptions parallel the federal laws and sometimes not. For example, California's salary test is $900 per month, and the definitions of the exempt categories vary somewhat from the FLSA. Some states have special industrial or job classification standards and exemptions, in addition to those provided by the FLSA.

Even though many states require overtime compensation to be paid for all hours over eight in one day, exceptions may be available under state law. One interesting exception available under California's regulations is where an employer, or his or her employees, wants to institute a 10-hour day, four days per week. If two-thirds of the affected employees agree in writing to such a workweek, the employer does not have to pay overtime for the ninth and tenth hours of each day as long as the employees have at least two days off between workweeks. Of course, if one or more of the employees works more than 40 hours in one week, or more than 10 hours in one day, the law requires payment of overtime compensation. Later, if two-thirds of the affected employees vote to curtail the 10-hour day, the employer must comply.

You may now conclude that wage and hour legislation and restrictions are intertwined, overlapping, and complex. They are. And, we have not touched on other related legislation such as the minimum wage and child labor laws. Where do you go for help? The U.S. Department of Labor or the local state employment office will provide informal advice. They will also send printed information upon request. There is also a procedure for requesting a formal written opinion from the applicable state agency or the local office of the U.S. Department of Labor, Wage and Hour Division.

The FLSA and state laws will require you to keep accurate and detailed employment records on wages or salary paid, hours worked, overtime paid, and deductions — to name a few. Contact your local wage and hour office (state and federal) for a detailed list of the records you must maintain and the length of time that you must preserve them. Also, see the **Comment** to the policy, Payroll Deductions, Section 390.

The law requires that nonexempt employees be paid overtime in applicable situations. The exempt employee is not so fortunate; however, nothing prevents you from providing your exempt employees with some recognition of overtime in appropriate circumstances.

A sample Overtime Approval Form follows the alternate policy statements.

Overtime Compensation Alternate Policy 1 350.1

Nonexempt salaried employees will be paid at the rate of one and one-half times their regular hourly rate of pay for all time worked in excess of 8 hours in any one day and 40 hours in any one workweek.

Note: *This statement assumes a state requirement for overtime after eight hours in one day.*

Overtime is never at the employee's discretion. It shall only be incurred and paid at the request of the company through the vice president.

Overtime Compensation Alternate Policy 2 350.2

Nonexempt employees will be paid at the rate of one and one-half times their regular rate of pay for the following:

1. Hours worked in excess of 8 and less than 12 in a single workday.

2. Hours worked in excess of 40 in a single workweek.

3. Hours worked on official company holidays.

Note: *Be sure to correlate this statement with your policy on holidays and holiday pay.*

Nonexempt employees will receive double their regular rate of pay for:

1. Hours worked in excess of 12 in a single workday.

2. Hours worked in excess of eight on the seventh workday and following consecutive workdays.

Note: *Again, state law on these matters is assumed, unless the employer desires this higher overtime pay even though no requirement exists.*

If a nonexempt employee receives shift premium, his or her regular rate of pay includes that premium.

Exempt employees may be eligible for overtime compensation, in appropriate circumstances, for hours worked in excess of a 40-hour workweek. However, managers are encouraged to recognize necessary exempt overtime by allowing compensatory time off to

Overtime Compensation — continued Alternate Policy 2 350.2

be taken at a time and under conditions mutually agreed upon between the exempt employee and his or her manager. Overtime compensation for exempt employees, other than compensatory time off, must be approved in advance by the (VICE PRESIDENT).

See general definitions of exempt and nonexempt employees, Employee Classifications, Section 240.

OVERTIME APPROVAL

______________________________ has approval to work overtime

on ____________________ (date) between the hours of ____________ and

____________.

______________________________ ____________
Supervisor's Signature Date

______________________________ ____________
Employee's Signature Date

Meal and Rest Periods 360

Comment: Both federal and state laws and regulations impact your company's meal and rest period policies. Often the state laws and regulations will parallel, and sometimes overlap, the federal. The federal law in question is the Fair Labor Standards Act (FLSA). It requires that all rest periods be paid time. Meal periods are not paid time if the employee is relieved of all of his or her duties. If the employee is required to eat at his or her desk or machine, then that time must be paid. A meal period of at least 30 minutes is sufficient, although shorter periods may qualify under special circumstances. The employer is not required to let the employee leave the premises for meals.

State laws and regulations must be researched to determine any additional standards, restrictions, or requirements in this area. Local law will prevail even if your business is not subject to the FLSA. For guidance regarding coverage, see the **Comment** to Overtime Compensation, Section 350. The following comments are based on California State Regulations which are probably representative of other states. But again, you should determine your specific local requirements and whether or not your business is subject to them.

Meal Period — If an employee works more than five hours, there must be at least a 30-minute meal period. The meal time need not be paid as long as the employee is relieved of all duties. The meal period can be waived by mutual consent of the employee and employer for employees working six hours or less per day.

Rest Period — There must be a rest period of at least 10 minutes for every four hours worked at the middle of each four-hour period. Employees working fewer than four hours per day are exempt from rest period requirements. There must be a 10-minute rest period for every two hours worked beyond the normal eight-hour shift. These rest periods are part of regular time worked or overtime hours, or both.

The following alternative policies suggest a 30-minute or an hour meal period and provide slight variations in the wording of the rest period policy.

Meal and Rest Periods Alternate Policy 1 360.1

Meal Period — The normal work day is eight hours, commencing at (ADD START TIME) and ending at (ADD CLOSING TIME) with a one-hour, unpaid lunch period beginning at noon.

Employees who begin their workday before noon and continue to work past 7:00 P.M. will be granted an unpaid 30-minute meal period between 5 P.M. and 7 P.M.

Rest Period — Nonexempt employees are permitted two paid 10-minute rest periods. Rest periods are to be scheduled as near the middle of the morning and afternoon as possible.

Meal and Rest Periods Alternate Policy 2 360.2

Meal Period — The required lunch period for all employees is 30 minutes. It may be taken at any time between 11 A.M. and 1:30 P.M. with the approval of the vice president.

Rest Period — Each employee is allowed two paid 10-minute rest periods, one for every four hours worked. For every two hours of overtime worked, an additional 10-minute rest period is allowed.

Flextime 370

Comment: "Flextime" has been introduced into the labor scene to allow employees more control over their work environment. It has many variations, some of which include flexible scheduling and compressed workweeks. Broadly defined, flextime is an arrangement established by management to allow employees to work fulltime at hours convenient to them.

Before you initiate flextime, consider the impact on management. It may be wise to allow your management team to decide if their workload or production schedule will be amenable to flextime. Next, the employees' opinions should be heard. You may consider instituting flextime for a trial period only, such as three or six months. Then evaluate both management and employee feedback to see if everyone's expectations are being met. If you desire to continue it, let the employees and their managers readjust their schedules if necessary, and repeat the whole process periodically.

Flextime is not for every company. Its greatest success has been in service companies rather than companies having a production line. Flextime reduces the hours a company or department will be fully staffed, but it expands the number of hours for service. Management's work time may be increased unless supervisors/managers coordinate their schedules to ensure supervisory coverage. Higher employee morale and an increase in the level of trust between employer and employee can outweigh these disadvantages. If your company adopts a flextime policy, you must ensure that company records accurately reflect the work time of each employee for purposes of the Fair Labor Standards Act as well as state law.

The flextime policies presented below are only two of several variations. One alternative is to let the employee and supervisor work out the employee's schedule giving consideration to that department's needs. A second alternative, although not flextime, is giving a few hours per week of merit or personal time off, with pay, and encouraging employees to use it for short personal absences, such as a doctor's appointment, or to make up for being late to work. Another alternative is a compressed schedule — four-day workweek and 10 hours per day. The Fair Labor Standards Act and many state labor laws or regulations will allow such a compressed schedule, without having to pay overtime, if a certain high percentage of employees vote for the schedule. These laws or regulations also give the employees the option to terminate it, again by a vote.

Flextime Alternate Policy 1 370.1

Flextime allows our employees optional starting and quitting times to coincide with their personal preference. The flextime employee is expected to be responsible and is trusted to begin and end work without direct supervision.

Available flextime schedules are as follows:

Begin Work	Conclude Work
8:00 A.M.	4:30 P.M.
8:15 A.M.	4:45 P.M.
8:30 A.M.	5:00 P.M.
8:45 A.M.	5:15 P.M.
9:00 A.M.	5:30 P.M.
9:15 A.M.	5:45 P.M.
9:30 A.M.	6:00 P.M.

The employee and vice president are to select a work schedule which ensures effective functioning of the company and is convenient to them.

Once a mutually convenient workday schedule has been chosen by the employee and vice president, the schedule becomes "fixed" and is to be adhered to without deviation. However, the employee normally may be allowed to change his or her schedule once every six months subject to the vice president's approval.

Flextime Alternate Policy 2 370.2

Employees are given the opportunity to schedule their own working hours within the limitations set by the company to meet its goals and objectives. The only requirement is that the fulltime employee must work eight hours each day and must arrive and leave within specified two-hour periods. Arrival time can be anytime between 6:30 A.M. and 8:30 A.M. Departure time can be anytime between 3:00 P.M. and 5:00 P.M. after eight hours of work.

Note: *This allows for a minimum of 30 minutes for lunch.*

The employee is expected to adhere to the general guidelines on a voluntary basis and to continue to meet job commitments and responsibilities. Another of the responsibilities is consideration of the needs of the work group and avoiding any disruption of others when arriving or departing from the work station. The employee must accurately fill out his or her time sheet each day. The vice president is responsible for fair administration of this flextime policy.

Performance Review and Salary Merit Increases 380

Comment: One of the most researched and discussed management concerns is an equitable and valid performance review process. Often in frustration, after lengthy management discussions on how to properly initiate a performance review process, the company will do nothing or implement a meaningless, vague, or subjective review process.

The challenge to your company is to establish a performance review process that is workable, equitable, ongoing, and as objective as possible. As your organization grows, it must be able to assess its individual and group achievements, as well as recognize and reward those individuals responsible for your company's success.

Performance reviews should provide employees with feedback on their performance. It should offer an opportunity for them to discuss ways of improving their performance and to discuss and establish future employment goals. For management, performance reviews can:

- Identify a need for employee or department training or both;
- Provide information for manpower and organizational planning;
- Reinforce or suggest modifications to the company employee selection process; and
- Improve employee morale when above average performance or extra effort is recognized and rewarded.

Research of the literature indicates that numerous techniques have been tested in search of a better method of performance appraisal. Some of the methods include:

- The narrative descriptive review where reviews are conducted in response to essay-type questions related to establishing and accomplishing specific employment goals;
- The rank method whereby employees in a work group are rank-ordered by some universal factor or factors, e.g., overall performance;
- A checklist or rating scale; and
- The management by objectives approach.

Federal legislation and court rulings, primarily in the equal employment opportunity area, have identified the following red flags to be aware of in considering your company performance appraisal process.

1. The rating criteria and standards selected must be job-related.

2. Supervisors/managers must have been able to consistently observe the employee in performing assigned tasks.

3. Supervisors/managers must use the same rating criteria.

4. Employees must be rated against standards rationally related to the group to which they functionally belong.

5. Criteria used in rating employees must not be vague or completely subjective and must not unfairly depress scores of protected classes, e.g., women, minorities, handicapped.

6. The importance of training your management team to conduct performance reviews should not be overlooked — all raters must understand what the rating criteria mean and have the interpersonal skills to effectively conduct the performance reviews.

Before management adopts any performance review process, there must be agreement on what standards will be used for ratings or performance appraisal. The process and standards must be fair and just to the employee as well as for the company. Communication, once again, is a key to the process: let your employees know what the process is and by what standards they will be measured. And allow them to make suggestions for improvement of both.

At a minimum, include the following information in your company policy:

- Criteria to be used in the performance review;
- How employee performance will be measured (against what standards);
- Who will do the appraisal(s);
- When the appraisal(s) will be done;
- What feedback will the employee receive;
- Can the employee give input to the process and when;
- What assistance will the company provide in improving performance; and
- The rewards for above average performance.

We further suggest that your company strive to establish a "coaching" relationship when initiating the performance review process. Although the performance review is intended to be a positive process, sometimes it is not. Every vice president must be encouraged to evaluate every employee accurately. Where an employee's performance is poor, the appraisal should so indicate, clearly and unequivocally. Substandard performance, or even average performance, should not be described in such a way that the employee believes that his or her performance is better than that. Emotions or time constraints must not be allowed to affect or undermine the review process. If an employee is terminated for poor performance, but all of his or her previous appraisals were good or vague, the employee may cause you great difficulty in a wrongful termination lawsuit.

Finally, there are many possible combinations of performance review policies and review forms which can be created. Which type of form will work best for you depends to a certain degree upon your management style and the nature of your employees. For example, a review process which focuses largely on planning goals and objectives may have little relevance to certain job categories, such as clerical or warehouse jobs. These employees may benefit more from a review process which focuses more immediately on productivity and evaluates such skills as quality and quantity of work produced, attitude, and teamwork.

Three alternate policies follow. Each of the alternate policies include a form for a review process which is closely tailored to the policy which precedes it. With minor language changes, however, any of the forms which follow could be adapted for use with any of the alternate policies. To minimize confusion to the reader, the form which follows Alternate Policy 1 is captioned Employee Work Plan and Performance Appraisal/Criteria for Appraising Demonstrated Performance. Following Alternate Policy 2, you will find a policy called Performance Appraisal. A form labeled Performance Review Outline follows Alternate Policy 3.

Performance Review and Salary Merit Increases Alternate Policy 1 380.1

Note: *If salary merit increases are not to be utilized in conjunction with performance reviews, the words "and salary merit increases" should be deleted.*

(COMPANY) has adopted a management by objectives approach to performance appraisal. Each employee is given the opportunity to set individual written goals. He or she will be evaluated based on how well these goals have been met. Three months after an employee joins the company, the vice president and employee will meet to establish employment goals consistent with the business objectives of the company and the employee's job responsibilities. The first performance review will occur near the end of the next three months, preferably on a date agreed to in writing. All future employee performance reviews will be scheduled at six month intervals and noted in the preceding appraisal report.

It is the company's responsibility to develop and maintain a work environment in which employees can openly discuss performance and develop plans. The employee will be notified in writing 10 days in advance of the performance review date. Also included in the notification will be the time, place, and the discussion topics for the employee to prepare for the review. The employee, as well as the vice president, is to bring the following to the review meeting:

1. A summary statement of the progress made toward meeting his or her employment goals;
2. Examples of job-related areas demonstrating greatest strengths and identifying areas where additional training is needed;
3. An outline of job-related tasks in which the employee can participate in to improve performance;

▶

4. A recommendation of job responsibilities and goals to be established for the next six-month period;
5. A summary of overall employment performance.

The Employee Work Plan and Performance Appraisal/Criteria for Appraising Demonstrated Performance form which follows this policy is to be used for the performance review. The Employee Work Plan and Performance Appraisal portion of this form serves as a planning tool by which employees and the vice presidents set forth specific examples of job performance. The Criteria for Appraising Demonstrated Performance portion of the form is used to evaluate overall employee performance based on the specific examples referred to on the Employee Work Plan and Performance Appraisal portion. Employees and the vice president should complete both portions of the form.

The vice president is responsible for establishing a relaxed atmosphere at the performance review and encouraging two-way communication. The discussion should be conducted in a positive manner, in complete privacy, and with no interruptions. The vice president shall verify that the employee is familiar with his or her job duties, previous goals, and the appraisal criteria or factors. At the conclusion of the performance appraisal, the employee will be requested to sign the appraisal verifying that he or she participated in the evaluation. The employee should be encouraged to submit comments about the appraisal which will become part of the record. A date for the next appraisal shall be agreed upon and noted on the appraisal form. The employee must be given a signed copy of the appraisal.

▶

Performance Review and Salary Merit Increases — continued Alternate Policy 1 380.1

(COMPANY) believes that pay increases should be related to an employee's performance. Following performance reviews, the vice president will rank the employee's performance according to his or her relative level of contribution to the company. Factors will include how well the employee has met the objectives agreed upon in the last review, whether it be the initial meeting or the following six-month review; and the employee's level of contribution to the success of the department/division relative to other employees. The vice president will rank all employees in one of four groupings:

1. Outstanding
2. Very Good
3. Good
4. Marginal

A decision relating to the employee's merit increase in pay will be made by the vice president after the review and ranking process has been completed. Any merit increase in pay will be retroactive to the date of performance appraisal. The vice president will forward a merit increase recommendation with the appraisal to the next level of management. Merit increases in pay are neither automatic nor periodic. They are reserved for employees who show skills improvement and higher than average performance.

Information pertaining to rates of pay and merit increases in pay, if any, are deemed to be confidential matters between the company and each employee and are not to be discussed among employees.

Note: *If performance or merit pay is not to be included, the three preceding paragraphs should be deleted.*

EMPLOYEE WORK PLAN AND PERFORMANCE APPRAISAL

(COMPANY) has adopted a management by objectives approach to performance reviews. Both employees and the vice president should respond in writing to the specific issues raised below prior to the scheduled review. Employees will be notified at least 10 days prior to the scheduled review. At the review, the employee and the vice president will discuss and compare each other's response to the issues. The first page should be considered a planning tool to prepare for the review session. Employees and the vice president should record specific examples of employee conduct and performance. The criteria listed on the reverse side is used to evaluate the employee's overall performance.

1. Major responsibilities of the job. ______________________________

____

2. Specific accomplishments since last performance appraisal. ______________________________

____

3. Specific examples of work quality. ______________________________

____

4. Specific examples of work quantity. ______________________________

____

5. Specific examples of employee's judgment in work performance. ______________________________

____

6. Specific examples of employee's initiative in completing assigned tasks. ______________________________

____

7. Specific examples of employee's teamwork with fellow employees. ______________________________

____

8. Specific examples of employee's dependability in completing tasks. ______________________________

____

9. Achievement of employee's goals. ______________________________

____

10. Summarize employee's performance. ______________________________

____

11. Action to be taken to improve performance. ______________________________

____

12. Employee's goals for next six months. ______________________________

____

13. Employee comments (employee may put additional comments on a separate sheet).

____

____

____

▶

CRITERIA FOR APPRAISING DEMONSTRATED PERFORMANCE

1. Work quality (reliability, accuracy, neatness of work) ______________________________
____
____

2. Work quantity (amount of work produced) ______________________________
____
____

3. Judgment (ability to make sound decisions in performing work tasks) ______________
____
____

4. Initiative (interest shown in job, dedication, willingness to complete tasks, and accept additional work) ______________________________
____
____

5. Teamwork (relationship with fellow employees in department/division) ______________
____
____

6. Dependability (reliability and responsiveness in completing assigned tasks) __________
____
____

7. Achievement of goals and objectives by employee (express as 100%, 50% etc). _______
____
____
____
____

I am signing this performance appraisal to indicate that my supervisor and I have met to discuss the above comments.

______________________________ ______________
Employee's Signature Date

______________________________ ______________
Vice President's Signature Date

Performance Review and Salary Merit Increases Alternate Policy 2 380.2

All employees of (COMPANY) will participate in a performance review with the vice president based on the following schedule:

1. Twice a year during (MONTH) and (MONTH)

Note: *Typically, the review should be approximately six months after employee is hired and every six to twelve months thereafter. Executive or management employees may only require a yearly review.*

2. As often as is warranted by the job situation and the employee's performance.

The performance review will be completed in writing after the completion of an interview between the employee and the vice president. The employee is encouraged to share in the review process by adding written comments to the evaluation form.

The employee is also encouraged to:

- Inquire about his or her performance from time to time;
- Accept additional responsibilities and show initiative;
- Review opportunities for advancement within the department or job classification;
- Ask for assistance in developing a goal-oriented path for advancement within the company;
- Learn about training available to assist the employee in skills improvement, promotion, or lateral transfer.

Performance Review and Salary Merit Increases — continued Alternate Policy 2 3090.2

The vice president will determine if a merit increase is warranted at the time of the performance review. It is (COMPANY) policy to reward employees with merit increases in salary for dedication in their work, extra effort, and better-than-average performance. Management does not award merit increases on an automatic basis or at any preset interval. All approved merit increases will be made retroactive to the first workday of the week of performance review.

Information pertaining to rates of pay and merit increases in pay, if any, are deemed to be confidential matters between the company and each employee and are not to be discussed among employees.

Note: *If performance or merit pay is not to be included, the preceding two paragraphs should be deleted.*

PERFORMANCE APPRAISAL

Employee's Name: ______________________________ Job Title: ____________________

Supervisor's Name: ____________________________ Performance Review Date: ________

The following scale should be used in evaluating the employee's performance when compared to the norm of his or her position. **Outstanding** - Employee consistently meets, and in many instances exceeds, established standards and desired results; **Very Good** - Employee consistently meets established standards; sometimes exceeds, and never falls short of desired results; **Satisfactory** - Employee meets established standards; usually meets and seldom falls short of desired results; and **Development Needed** - Employee meets established standards in some instances but lacks consistency; seldom exceeds and frequently falls short of desired results from time to time.

	Out-standing	Very Good	Satis-factory	Develop-ment Needed	Comments
Performs Job Skills:					
Knowledge of Work:					
Ability to Organize:					
Quality of Work:					
Quantity of Work:					
Communication:					
Teamwork:					
Meets Deadlines:					
Dependability:					
Judgment:					
Attitude:					
Problem Solving:					

Areas needing improvement: ____

____

____

Areas where improvement has been made: _____________________________

____

____

Objectives met since last review: ___________________________________

____

____

Objectives set for next evaluation period: ______________________________

____

____

Summary of evaluation: ______________________________________

____

____

____

____

Employee comments: (Separate sheet may be attached.) ____________________

____

____

____

____

____

______________________________________ ______________
Employee's Signature Date

______________________________________ ______________
Vice President's Signature Date

The following definitions should assist you in completing the Performance Appraisal Form:

Term	**Definition**
Performs Job Skills	Ability to perform assigned job tasks.
Knowledge of Work	Technical knowledge of job and related work.
Ability to Organize	Effectiveness in planning own work.
Quality of Work	Accuracy of work; freedom form errors.
Quantity of Work	Output of work; speed.
Communication	Effective communication with manager and others.
Teamwork	Ability to work together within the department.
Meets Deadlines	Timeliness in performing work; deadlines.
Dependability	Reliability in carrying out assignments conscientiously.
Judgment	Ability to obtain and analyze facts and apply sound judgement.
Attitude	Positive attitude and enthusiasm to work and others.
Problem Solving	Ability to develop more efficient means to job tasks.

Performance Review and Salary Merit Increases Alternate Policy 3 380.3

All employees will participate in a performance review process that has been initiated as a company-wide system. The system provides greater employee participation in personal growth and a greater degree of employee self-management. Thirty days after each employee joins (COMPANY), the employee will draft objectives to be met in the position within the next 90 days. The vice president will complete a similar list, and the two will meet and agree on the performance objectives to be achieved at the end of 120 days. An important part of this performance planning will be prioritizing the objectives. The employee or vice president may request an interim progress review at anytime during the following 90 days.

The 120-day evaluation shall consist of reviewing results and achievements against the established objectives, reviewing the priorities, and establishing the next set of objectives for future evaluations. The focus for the evaluation will be on how closely the employee is meeting his or her potential in the assigned position. The required terminology to be used in the evaluation will be "exceeded," "achieved," or "below" with respect to the standards set in the defined objectives.

Here are some performance factors that should be considered in the development of employee objectives:

- Organizational skill
- Planning skill
- Decision making
- Job commitment
- Knowledge of field
- Communications
- Teamwork

PERFORMANCE REVIEW OUTLINE

All employees participate in a company-wide review process. Prior to each review, both the employee and the vice president will draft responses to the criteria described below. The review will consist in part of a comparison of the responses prepared by the employee and the vice president. Both parties will also work together to develop new objectives and priorities to achieve prior to the next scheduled review.

Employee Objectives:

1. ______________________________
2. ______________________________
3. ______________________________

Results to Achieve: ______________________________

____

Priorities: ______________________________

____

Interim Review (list dates):

1. ______________________________
2. ______________________________
3. ______________________________

Change in Objectives: ______________________________

____

Change in Priorities: ______________________________

____

Performance Evaluation: ______________________________

____

Results and Achievements: ______________________________

____

New Objectives and Priorities: ______________________________

____

Next Review Date: ______________________________

______________________________ ______________
Employee's Signature Date

______________________________ ______________
Vice President's Signature Date

Payroll Deductions 390

Comment: As an employer, you have certain obligations to federal, state, and local governments regarding the withholding of taxes from the salaries of your employees and the payment of various payroll taxes to the government. Your obligations, the procedures to be followed, and the reporting requirements imposed are discussed in IRS *Circular E, Employer's Tax Guide*. The state and local jurisdictions have their own publications describing requirements and procedures.

Federal income taxes are withheld on all wages paid to an employee above a certain minimum. This minimum is governed by the number of withholding allowances claimed by the employee on IRS *Form W-4*. Every employee is required to fill out a *W-4*. Social Security taxes apply to all wages earned by an employee during a year up to a maximum amount. This amount and the tax rate increase from year to year, so you need to check the current amount and the rate each year. The percentage deduction from the employee's wages is matched by an additional tax paid by the employer. Federal unemployment taxes are paid by the employer based on a set formula. The rates vary from time to time with new legislation. As an employer, you are, in effect, an agent of the government in collecting income, Social Security, and federal unemployment taxes. This is also true for state and city income taxes and any other state or local employment tax, such as disability insurance. Bear in mind that any officer or other executive who has the responsibility to withhold and pay these taxes, and fails to do so, may become personally liable for the taxes, if the company cannot pay. This obligation is aggressively enforced!

Every employee should receive an itemized written statement from the employer for every pay period. The statement should contain all of the information specified in the **Comment** to Workday, Payday and Pay Advances, Sections 320–40. Every employer who withholds taxes is also required to provide every employee with an annual Wage and Tax Statement — *Form W-2* — for the calendar year. The *W-2* must be provided to each employee by January 31st of the following year, or earlier if the employee terminates. Copies of all employee *W-2*'s, including a summary form *(W-3)*, must be filed with the IRS by the last day of February. Usually, the state or local jurisdiction will allow combined reporting of applicable state or local deductions using the federal forms.

You should also report other employee payroll deductions which relate to the company fringe benefit package, if these costs are paid by the employee.

A policy is usually necessary to explain to your employees the types of deductions that will be made from their payroll check. You should also refer to any voluntary deductions for contributions to a stock plan, pension plan, or credit union, if applicable to your company.

Payroll Deductions 390.1

The following mandatory deductions will be made from every employee's gross wages: federal income tax, Social Security FICA tax, and applicable city and state taxes.

Every employee must fill out and sign a federal withholding allowance certificate, IRS *Form W-4*, on or before his or her first day on the job. This form must be completed in accordance with federal regulations. The employee may fill out a new *W-4* at anytime when his or her circumstances change. Employees who paid no federal income tax for the preceding year and who expect to pay no income tax for the current year may fill out an *Exemption From Withholding Certificate*, IRS *Form W-4E*. Employees are expected to comply with the instructions on *Form W-4*. Questions regarding the propriety of claimed deductions may be referred to the IRS in certain circumstances.

Every employee will receive an annual *Wage and Tax Statement, IRS Form W-2*, for the preceding year on or before January 31. Any employee who believes that his or her deductions are incorrect for any pay period, or on *Form W-2*, should check with (COMPANY) immediately. Your vice president will give you time to do this during the workday.

Footnotes

320–40 — Workday, Payday, and Pay Advances

1. Cal. Lab. Code § 204.
2. Cal. Lab. Code § 207.
3. 29 C.F.R. § 516.2(a).

Chapter 4
Employee Benefits and Expenses

Introduction/Benefits

Once known as fringe benefits — accounting for 2% to 3% of the payroll cost — employee benefits today can no longer be considered fringe. Their security and nontax advantages are significant to the employee; their cost is significant to the employer. Many employees view the benefits package as a matter of entitlement with no appreciation of the costs involved. Employers should endeavor to make employees aware of the cost of these programs.

In the development of the company employee benefit program, the challenge is to provide a package of policies which will enhance employee morale and lead to greater productivity. Obviously, you have to pay for these objectives. Employee benefit packages today frequently exceed 50% of direct labor cost, and this rate is projected to climb steadily over the coming years. However, the cost is justifiable if for no other reason than the resulting high morale and greater productivity.

Another challenge to your organization is keeping abreast of the types of benefits provided by other companies and updating your benefit package to provide an attractive and competitive compensation program. Present day employees are better educated, better informed, and more aware of economic incentives than in previous years. They want and expect to share their views and opinions with management. Also, times of inflation and relatively high mobility tend to increase the communication among employees in comparing benefit packages from company to company. Therefore, you should consider a survey of your present employees to determine their opinions and preferences about the types of benefits potentially available. Creativity and flexibility in the development of benefit programs will provide a strong allegiance between the company and its employees. Company-provided benefits and services can be used as an important marketing tool to attract and retain quality personnel.

The compensation package developed for middle management employees is usually comprised of the same benefits received by their subordinates, and there also tends to be some trickling down of benefits from top management. Remember, however, that exempt middle management employees share a considerable amount of the responsibility for a company's success but do not share in the same benefits which top management reserves for itself. There appears to be some justification to recognize middle management's contribution in ways other than what the nonexempt employee has come to expect.

Here are some of the compensation alternatives you might consider for exempt employees:

- Larger amounts of life insurance proportional to base pay
- Opportunities to attend professional meetings
- Receipt of company subscriptions to professional newspapers, magazines, and journals
- Occasional use of a company car
- Special parking places
- Club memberships
- Free tickets to entertainment events
- Use of special corporate entertainment facilities
- Bonus plans
- Time off or use of company resources, or both, to write a paper for presentation to a professional organization
- Opportunities to select special challenging organizational assignments
- Opportunities to take a guest to professional meetings at company expense
- Stock options
- Free child care or child care allowance

Employers that provide certain benefits to their employees will have to comply with the requirements of the Employee Retirement Income Security Act, commonly known as ERISA. The act deals with two kinds of employee benefit plans: pension plans and welfare plans. Pension plans include tax-qualified retirement plans, profit-sharing plans, employee stock ownership plans (ESOPs) and individual retirement accounts (IRAs). Welfare plans include health insurance, long-term disability, group life, and accidental death insurance plans.

A related issue to be considered is what benefits, if any, are to be provided to your sales staff. Often times, this issue is preceded by a determination of whether your sales staff is considered to be employees or independent contractors. Employees are generally eligible for some or all of the benefits made available to other company employees; independent contractors are not. Although the key determinant is the amount of control exercised by the employer, each state imposes its own tests for unemployment and workers' compensation purposes. Check with your legal adviser to develop a policy which will work best for you.

Policies relating to employee benefits are found in Sections 400 through 420.

Introduction/Expenses

Company policies respecting employee expenses are necessary to support the following:

- To efficiently carry out business assignments, an employee may sometimes be required to make personal expenditures on behalf of the company;
- Your employees' educational and professional growth through organizational memberships, attendance at conferences or seminars, and enrolling in higher education courses;
- Relocation assistance for new or transferred employees.

In developing this section of your policy manual, you will want to achieve a balance between what your company can afford and what other companies — primarily your competition — are providing for their employees. As you look at the competition, however, consider the nonmonetary, as well as the monetary, benefits of the policies in this section. Does your company provide:

- A challenging work environment where people like to work;
- Activities or facilities to release job stress;
- The opportunity for association and interaction with highly-skilled and talented co-workers; and
- Opportunities for employee development and education?

In today's society where employees are asking for a higher quality work environment, these factors often rate above any monetary benefits or salary. It is not only important to address these four factors in your policies, but it is also important to stress in employee orientation meetings that they are benefits which your company provides.

Employee expense policies should be written with greater flexibility than other policies. Although flexibility is an important aspect of these policies, consider, however, these two points as well: they do provide important management and budget consistency; and without a policy, these employee expenses and benefits could easily absorb available and necessary operational and marketing funds.

Policies pertaining to employee expenses are found in Sections 430 through 450.

Vacation 400

Comment: Vacations are an integral part of the overall fringe benefit package. Although vacation policies vary widely, the trend in recent years has been to liberalize vacation entitlements. Many organizations provide a vacation package similar to this:

- One week after six months to one year of service;
- Two weeks after one to three years of service;
- Three weeks after three to ten years of service;
- Four weeks after ten years of service.

Vacations provide employees with paid time away from their jobs to afford them an opportunity for recreation, rest, and relaxation. To minimize the disruptive effect of many employees requesting vacation in the summer months, companies may consider offering a bonus (e.g., $50) for each week of vacation taken in months other than May through September. Another innovative idea to consider is a vacation banking plan, enabling employees to trade all or part of their unused vacation for a cash equivalent, which is collected at the end of the year, upon termination, or upon retirement from the organization. The argument against this plan is that employees should be encouraged to take their vacation so that job burn-out and absenteeism for health-related reasons are avoided and productivity and safety are promoted. Some employers actually state their preference for employee vacations in their policies.

Federal law does not require employers to provide "vested" vacation time or even paid vacations. Some states, by law, may require a certain minimum vacation time — paid or unpaid — or even a permanent credit for vacation time not taken (vesting). But generally, the right to paid vacation time, whether or not the time is vested, arises as a result of an employment contract, a collective bargaining agreement, or the company's policy. Some states recognize paid vacation time as a form of deferred wages and consider it vested in proportion to length of service. In those states, paid vacation time not taken by the employee, just like final wages, must be paid to a terminating employee. Likewise, an employer may be prohibited by state law from enforcing a policy of forfeiture of vested vacation pay.[1] You should consult your state law for such provisions.

Virtually every employer provides paid vacation, and many employers have a policy for vesting. Variations exist, however, as to when the vacation time is actually earned — anniversary date, beginning of the calendar or company fiscal year, per pay period. The date that paid vacation is actually earned, and whether or not it is vested, is oftentimes an issue when an employee terminates and demands payment for paid vacation time not taken. Draft your vacation policies clearly and specify exactly when an employee's vacation entitlement is earned. However, this may still not protect you from having to pay terminating employees for pro rata vacation not taken if your state prohibits forfeiture of vested vacation pay.

In some industries, vacation plans are "funded," and employers are required to pay a set amount into a trust fund set up to provide paid vacation time. If this applies to a particular employer, he or she is required by law to make these payments or suffer a penalty. These types of funded vacation plans are subject to ERISA, and state law should be consulted for additional requirements.

Alternate policies are provided in this section. The first provides for a three-month waiting period before any vacation may be taken. Each policy presents variations in both accrual rates and carryover of earned vacation days into the next year. The authors cannot guarantee that either policy will protect you from having to pay terminating employees for vacation not taken. That depends on your state law.

An alternative paragraph which clearly provides for vested vacation time is provided after Alternate Policy 2. It can be used, with modifications, in either policy model.

A sample Leave Request Form follows the alternate policies. The Leave Request Form provides a tracking for accounting of leave taken by company employees.

Vacation Alternate Policy 1 400.1

Vacation benefits are based on the employee's next anniversary date which occurs in the current calendar year. The schedule is as follows:

Anniversary Date in Calendar Year	Vacation Entitlement as of January 1 of Calendar Year
1st through 4th	2 weeks
5th through 9th	3 weeks
10th through 19th	4 weeks
20th through 24th	5 weeks
25th or more	6 weeks

The employee's anniversary date is established according to the policy in Section 2100. To be eligible to take vacation, the employee must be in active pay status. Vacation is not vested, and a terminating employee will not be paid for vacation not taken. Vacation not taken during the calendar year is forfeited.

Note: *The preceding two sentences are optional and may conflict with state law and should be researched.*

New employees become eligible to take vacation after they have worked three consecutive months. Those reporting on the first working day in January are entitled to two weeks of paid vacation. Those reporting after the first working day in January through the first working day in July are entitled to one week of paid vacation. New employees reporting for work

Vacation— continued Alternate Policy 1 400.1

after the first working day in July are not entitled to paid vacation until the following year. Part-time employees are not entitled to paid vacation. Employees who are not entitled to paid vacation may request permission from the vice president to take up to one week of unpaid vacation time.

The vice president is responsible for scheduling vacations. Normally, two-weeks advance notice of vacation is expected and necessary to ensure scheduling of work. Employees who desire to take more than three weeks of vacation at one time should give the vice president more than two weeks advance notice.

Vacation Alternate Policy 2 400.2

Vacation accrual begins with the first month of hire. Monthly accrual rates are determined by the employee's anniversary date, according to the schedule that follows. A new employee accrues the entire 6.67 hours of vacation time for the first month of service regardless of the day of the month the employee is hired. An employee must be in active pay status on the last working day of the month to accrue vacation for that month.

Vacation time accrues at a rate of 6.67 hours each month of fulltime service (10 days for every 12 months) up through the first five years of continuous employment. Accrual rates thereafter are as follows:

Years Completed	Hours Accrued per Month	Yearly Total
5	10.00	15 days
15	13.34	20 days
20	15.00	22.5 days
25 and over	16.67	25 days

If the employee's 5th, 15th, 20th, or 25th anniversary date is on or before the last working day of the month, the employee will accrue the higher rate for that month. Vacation is not earned while an employee is on a leave of absence. Part-time employees earn vacation at half the accrual rates above.

Employees may take total "available" vacation at any time throughout the year. All vacations must be scheduled in advanced with the vice president.

Employees may carry over accrued vacation, but all vacation hours carried over from one calendar year must be used by the end of the following year, or they will be forfeited.

Note: *This last sentence may conflict with state law and should be researched.*

Vesting Clause Alternative 400.3

An employee's vacation time vests when it is accrued and can be carried over to future calendar years if not taken. This means that the earned vacation is permanently credited to the employee. An employee cannot take more than 25 consecutive days of vacation (excluding Saturdays, Sundays, and holidays) in any one calendar year without the approval of the (VICE PRESIDENT). Upon termination, the employee's accrued, but not taken vacation hours, will be added to the final paycheck using the employee's then current, straight-time hourly rate for conversion.

LEAVE REQUEST FORM

______________________________ ______________
Name Date

Type of Leave: ☐ Annual ☐ Sick ☐ Holiday ☐ Leave without pay

Start: day ______________ date ______________ time ______________

End: day ______________ date ______________ time ______________

Total hours: ______________

______________________________ ______________
Approved by Date

Holidays 410

Comment: This policy designates the number of holidays which will be observed by the company and explains related scheduling and pay practices. Most companies now provide employees with 9 to 12 paid holidays a year. The most commonly observed holidays for federal employees are: New Year's Day, Martin Luther King, Jr.'s Birthday, Presidents Day, Memorial Day, Independence Day, Labor Day, Columbus Day, Veterans Day, Thanksgiving Day, and Christmas Day. Other holidays to be considered might include Good Friday, Presidential Election Day, and an additional day at Thanksgiving and Christmas. States have various special state holidays, and local statutes and regulations should be consulted prior to selecting the company holidays.

Two alternative policies are presented in this section, one providing specific holidays and a second providing the employee with a choice of floating holidays, in addition to specific company holidays. Specific dates can be identified by a company memorandum issued once a year to every employee, or the policy itself can be modified year by year.

Holidays Alternate Policy 1 410.1

(COMPANY) provides (ADD NUMBER) paid holidays each year. The company is officially closed on these days:

Note: *Select from or add to the paid holidays listed below.*

January 1*	New Year's Day
February	President's Day
March/April	Good Friday
May	Memorial Day
July	Independence Day
September	Labor Day
October	Columbus Day
November	Thanksgiving Day
November	Day after Thanksgiving
December 24th**	Christmas Eve (office closes at 12 noon)
December 25th*	Christmas Day
December 31st**	New Year's Eve (office closes at 12 noon)

*If these holidays fall on Saturday, the preceding Friday will be a holiday. If they fall on Sunday, the following Monday will be a holiday.

**If these holidays fall on weekends, one-half day off will be observed on the last work day preceding the holiday.

Holidays Alternate Policy 2 410.2

(COMPANY) provides 10 designated paid holidays each year. Eight of these are scheduled and identified on the company bulletin board, and two are "floating" holidays to be determined by the employee and approved by his or her supervisor. The eight scheduled holidays are as listed below:

Note: *Tailor number of designated paid and floating holidays to your specific policy.*

New Year's Day
Martin Luther King Jr.'s Birthday
Memorial Day
Independence Day
Labor Day
Thanksgiving
Day after Thanksgiving
Christmas

Weekend Holidays

When a recognized holiday falls on a Saturday, it will be observed on the Friday before the holiday. Recognized holidays that fall on a Sunday will be observed on the following Monday.

Eligibility for Holiday Pay

Employees must work the last scheduled day before a holiday and the first scheduled working day following the holiday to be eligible for holiday pay unless time off on these days has been excused with pay (e.g., vacation and sick leave). Only regular fulltime employees are eligible for full holiday pay. Temporary employees are not eligible for holiday pay.

Holidays — continued Alternate Policy 2 410.2

Part-time employees are entitled to an equal number of company holidays, but they shall receive pay for only the number of hours they would have regularly worked. Scheduled work on holidays is discouraged since the purpose of holidays is seen by the company as a provision for employee relaxation. If an employee is required to work on a scheduled holiday, the employee will be paid for hours worked at his or her regular pay in addition to holiday pay.

If a designated holiday falls within an employee's vacation period, the holiday is not considered a vacation day.

Employees may take religious holidays not designated as a company holiday either as a floating holiday or without pay. Prior approval in advance must be obtained from the vice president.

Sick or Personal Leave 420

Comment: Companies recognize an employee's need for income protection to reduce the financial burden during temporary periods of sickness or injury. Many companies which provide sick or personal leave, stress in the policy or new employee orientation that, unlike vacation leave, sick leave is not earned by the employee but is granted. Whether it is called "sick leave" or "personal leave," the time is generally thought of by employers as being provided for an employee who is temporarily incapacitated, not free time just because it is provided in the benefit package. Some companies allow an employee to take personal leave without being incapacitated, but limit the number of consecutive days of leave, e.g., five consecutive days during a twelve-month period. To encourage employees not to abuse this privilege, a number of innovative ideas are offered by companies, such as allowing an employee who has not used sick or personal leave during the year to receive paid leave time between the Christmas–New Year's holidays, or allowing an employee with perfect attendance during the month to receive an extra day's pay for that month (sometimes referred to as well pay). Other organizations buy back unused sick leave time at the end of the year by paying their employees for each day of sick leave not used. Some companies also vest sick or personal leave and will allow the employee to accumulate all unused portions of this leave to be ultimately cashed out if and when the employee terminates. Although federal law does not require sick or personal leave, state law may regulate this area or specify certain minimum entitlements.

Employees are more likely to call in sick when they believe that their attendance does not matter, when working conditions are stressful, or when they feel taken for granted. The company's attention to the following points in administering a sick leave policy will have a positive effect on attendance.

- Ensure that all employees know the sick leave policy and that the company sticks to the policy.
- Managers should set the company example: coming to work in spite of allergies or a sprained wrist will let employees know that the same level of commitment is expected from them.
- Employees calling in sick should be required to talk directly to their supervisor or a company officer. The supervisor or officer can stress that they will be missed and express hope that they will recover quickly. An employee who is required to talk directly to a supervisor or officer in such a case is more likely to have a good reason for calling in sick.
- Supervisors or officers should talk with employees following absenteeism to reinforce that they were missed. Such personal attention is important for team spirit.
- Encourage employees who are feeling pressure or stress on the job to talk to their supervisor about it. Encourage supervisors to be better listeners.

Small companies encounter higher costs because of employee absenteeism: they usually pay sick leave for that day and someone else must assume two persons' responsibilities or work goes undone. Creative incentive programs for perfect employee attendance for a six-month, one-year, or two-year program might include cash bonuses, vacation trips, or dollar credits to purchase merchandise from a catalog.

Sometimes sick leave is combined with vacation (becoming earned and vested) and called time off with pay. This time is then available to the employee in his or her discretion with a supervisor's approval.

Sick or Personal Leave Alternate Policy 1 420.1

A regular fulltime employee will receive 40 hours of sick leave after six months of continuous employment. A regular part-time employee will be credited with an appropriate prorated number of hours. After the first six months of employment, sick leave is accrued monthly at a rate of 6.67 hours for a fulltime employee and at a prorated amount for a part-time employee. Sick leave is accrued on the last workday of the month. Employees must be in an active pay status on the last day of the month to accrue sick leave for that month.

It is in the best interests of an employee who is ill or injured that the employee not remain at work. It is the vice president's responsibility to send the employee home if the employee is incapacitated.

Time for routine doctor or dentist appointments is not to be charged to sick leave. Employees are encouraged to make such appointments before arriving for work or after leaving work for the day, if possible. If time off is required for such appointments, arrangements should be made in advance with the vice president.

The employee must use accumulated sick leave in conjunction with income protection plans or other sources of disability income to achieve full pay for as long as possible. However, at no time can the combination of these exceed normal earnings.

An employee is expected to notify the vice president at the beginning of each work day during illness or injury. Exceptions to this include a serious accidental injury, hospitalization, and when it is known in advance that the employee will be absent for a certain period of time.

▶

Sick or Personal Leave — continued Alternate Policy 1 420.1

A Medical Release Statement is to be submitted to the vice president for review before the employee returns to work in the following situations:

1. Five or more consecutive work days of absence due to illness or injury;
2. In all cases of work-related injury when the employee has been unable to work after the time of the injury; or
3. When returning from medical or maternity leave of absence.

In the case of a work-related accident or injury, the company will compensate an employee for any lost work hours beginning on the date of the accident or injury and for the next (ADD NUMBER) hours of scheduled work time lost as a result of that accident or injury. The employee's sick leave is not to be used for this purpose. The employee must then use accumulated sick leave in conjunction with worker's compensation or other disability income to achieve full pay for as long as possible. However, at no time can the combination of these exceed normal earnings.

Unused sick leave will be forfeited upon termination. No employee will be allowed to overdraw sick leave beyond (ADD NUMBER) hours without approval in writing from the (VICE PRESIDENT). Such approval will only be granted on the condition, in writing and signed by the employee, that overdrawn sick leave will be deducted from the employee's final paycheck upon termination.

Sick leave is not earned while an employee is on a leave of absence.

Sick or Personal Leave Alternate Policy 2 420.2

Sick or personal leave equivalent to 10 days per year, earned at a rate of 6.67 hours per month, is granted to all fulltime employees. Part-time employees will earn sick or personal leave at half of the fulltime rate. Temporary employees are not eligible for sick or personal leave.

Sick leave is earned on the last workday of the month for all employees on active pay status that day. An employee beginning employment earns the entire 6.67 hours of sick or personal leave for the first month, regardless of when he or she starts work. An employee who is on leave of absence does not earn sick leave.

Sick or personal leave is vested by the company on behalf of the employee as it is earned. This means that the leave is permanently credited to the employee, and the dollar equivalent of any unused leave will be paid to the employee when, and if, he or she leaves the company. The vested leave time payout may not exceed a total of four months equivalent salary for the employee.

Note: *The last sentence is optional and may conflict with state law and should be researched.*

If it is necessary for an employee to request sick or personal leave in excess of the amount earned, the vice president has the authority to approve up to 40 hours in excess of the accrued amount. All excess sick or personal leave will be applied toward the employee's future accrual of sick or personal leave. The dollar equivalent of sick or personal leave owed to the company will be deducted from the employee's final check when an employee terminates.

Note: *Some states may require a previously-written authorization for this deduction signed by the employee prior to granting excess sick leave.*

Sick or Personal Leave — continued Alternate Policy 2 420.2

An employee is to contact the vice president when sick or personal leave is needed because of illness. It remains the employee's responsibility to keep the vice president informed as to his or her condition and when he or she will return to work. A medical statement from the employee's doctor may be requested by the company when an employee is absent from work for more than five working days.

Employee-Incurred Expenses and Reimbursement 430

Comment: Most businesses will want to consider the development of a policy to reimburse employees for out-of-pocket expenses which are necessary for the performance of company business.

The availability of an in-house purchasing department, the establishment of charge accounts with local businesses, or a procedure for submitting requests to the supervisor/manager on a set day each week for necessary supplies or materials may answer the need for a reimbursement policy for a company with less than 20 employees. As the number of employees increases, it becomes more important to place greater control on these expenditures. However, it may still be necessary for employees to use their own money for small, extraordinary purchases and when on travel status.

At a minimum, here are some actions you will want to take:

- Design a form to be used in requesting advance approval of company-related expenditures;
- Establish procedures and controls for your management team to follow in approving such requests;
- Design an expense report form for use in all cases of employee reimbursement; and
- Establish a procedure for submitting and approving expense reports and reimbursing the employee.

Employers who have state and federal government contracts or subcontracts subject to specific cost accounting guidelines, such as Cost Accounting Standards, should probably be more detailed in their definitions of reimbursable expenses. It is to your advantage to use language taken directly from such guidelines in defining a proper, reasonable, and allowable expense. A reference in the policy to governmental standards for reimbursable expenses is also helpful in those cases where a question arises concerning whether or not a particular expense is allowable. You may still want to reimburse the employee for a reasonable and necessary expense and assume the risk that it might not be recoverable.

The Tax Reform Act of 1986 has made some changes in how entertainment expenses will be allowed as deductions. Without going into detail (your CPA or tax counsel should advise you), generally only 80% of your business entertainment expenses will be deductible. These expenses are allowed only if they can be shown to be directly related to or associated with the active conduct of a trade or business; therefore, it is now important to break out these expenses on an expense report for later segregation and reporting. Also, you may need to pay attention to your entertainment expenses at clubs or associations which discriminate against races or by sex. Recent regulations and statutes may deny deductibility of such entertainment. Ask your tax expert.

It is worthwhile to consider implementing a rule within this policy, and probably within other employee reimbursement policies, that the expense report or reimbursement form be submitted to the appropriate approval authority, such as the accounting department, within a certain period of time. Some companies require the employee to submit a form within one or two weeks or five to ten business days after the expenditure. This kind of rule encourages the employee to submit a time report when dates and times are more easily recalled. It also ensures that expenses will be properly allocated to the company's fiscal quarter or year without having to adjust closing entries. A stale report is often an inaccurate report, and inaccuracies can cause disapprovals and misunderstandings which lead to poor morale. Obviously, enforcement of the rule must be tempered with some flexibility for an unusual situation, such as when an employee loses his or her briefcase and must reconstruct the itinerary and obtain duplicate receipts.

Some companies do take a very firm stand on timely reports. For instance, all reports which are 30 or 60 days late will be disapproved. Likewise, the company has a responsibility to provide the employee reimbursement promptly. Again, this is an issue affecting morale and your policy should reflect this duty to return to the employee the money that is rightfully his or hers without delay.

Employee-Incurred Expenses and Reimbursement Alternate Policy 1 430.1

To ensure that all proper business-related expenses incurred by employees are reimbursed, the following procedure has been established:

1. All expenditures are to be approved in advance by the vice president unless circumstances prevent advance approval.
2. All business-related expenditures must be accompanied by a receipt or evidence of expenditure in order to receive reimbursement.
3. All items purchased or charged by the employee are to be itemized on the approved company expense report. All portions of the report must be filled out or marked "N/A" (not applicable), and the necessity and purpose of the expenditure must be explained in sufficient detail.
4. Expense reports must be signed and dated by the employee. Reports are due within 30 days of the expenditure. Reimbursement will be made by the fifth working day of the month following submittal of the expense report.

Employee–Incurred Expenses and Reimbursement Alternate Policy 2 430.2

(COMPANY) will pay all actual and reasonable business-related expenses incurred by employees in the performance of their job responsibilities. All such expenses incurred by an employee must be approved by his or her manager before payment will be made by the accounting department.

Expense reports are to be submitted and supported by evidence of proof of purchase, e.g., receipts. Expense reports are due in the (ACCOUNTING DEPARTMENT) the last working day of each month.

Mileage Reimbursement 440

Comment: When an employee is asked to use his or her personal vehicle in conducting company business, the employer should reimburse the employee for such trips. The use of personal vehicles to run company business errands, such as to the post office or office supply store, may start out as a casual request. But later the employee may be asked to contribute many dollars out of his or her pocket considering today's gasoline prices and other auto-related expenses. To avoid any questions or misunderstandings, you should establish a policy to specify the conditions under which such reimbursement will be made. Of course, you could adopt a policy which discourages use of personal vehicles for company-related trips. Some companies allow or require employees to use the company-owned vehicle for such trips.

The policy should establish:

- The rate of reimbursement;
- The definition of what constitutes company travel;
- A rule on whether or not reporting to work prior to company travel is required;
- The method to be used to calculate miles traveled;
- The company's policy relating to insurance; and
- The procedure to follow to request mileage reimbursement.

As a general rule, employers will be liable to third parties injured as a result of an accident caused by an employee on company-related business. This is probably true even if the employee uses his or her personal vehicle without being required to do so by the employer, as long as the employer knew or should have known of the employee's use of a personal vehicle. The employer's liability to the employee for his or her personal injuries in such a situation is governed by state workers' compensation law. What is not clear, state to state, is whether the employer is liable to the employee for damage to the employee's vehicle. This issue depends on the facts, and especially, whether the employer required the personal vehicle to be used and the level of the employee's negligence in driving. Therefore, the employer should consider the value of employees using their personal vehicles against the potential liability involved. An attorney should be consulted for answers to specific questions regarding liability in such situations. Also, the employer who adopts a policy permitting personal vehicle use should consult the company liability insurer regarding coverage of employees and their vehicles. It is also wise to state in your policy that use of a personal vehicle is for the employee's convenience, or words to that effect. However, this is no guarantee that your liability for your employee's negligence will be prevented. Never require use of personal vehicles, or else the liability becomes more certain. An employer should also take steps to determine, or require a written statement, that the employee has a valid driver's license and maintains satisfactory liability insurance prior to using a personal vehicle for company business purposes. Keep in mind that many personal insurance policies do not provide coverage for accidents occurring while making business use of an automobile.

If no mileage reimbursement is to be provided, employees may elect to compute and deduct actual auto expenses or deduct mileage at a rate of 26 cents per mile subject, of course, to the rules and regulations of the Internal Revenue Code. If the standard mileage rate is used, no separate deduction is available to employees for depreciation, maintenance and repairs, tires, gasoline (including gasoline taxes), oil, insurance, and registration fees.

Mileage Reimbursement Alternate Policy 1 440.1

For the convenience of the employee, when he or she desires to use his or her personal vehicle for company business, all employees of (COMPANY) shall be reimbursed for company-related business travel at the rate of (ADD DOLLAR AMOUNT) per mile. Use of a personal vehicle is never required by the company and is discretionary on the part of the employee.

Travel expenses between your home and your assigned work location are not reimbursable. If an employee is required to travel from home directly to a third location on company business and then to work, the company will reimburse the employee for the difference between the mileage the employee normally drives to work and the total miles driven for business purposes.

Requests for reimbursement of business-related travel will be submitted to the vice president for approval on a standard company expense report. Reimbursement requests will include the following:

1. Date of travel
2. Beginning and ending odometer readings for each trip
3. Travel destination
4. Number of miles traveled on company business
5. The reason for company travel

The expense report must be signed and dated by the employee. The reports must be submitted to the vice president and will be processed according to the policy, Employee-Incurred Expenses and Reimbursement, Section 430.

Mileage Reimbursement — continued Alternate Policy 1 440.1

The employee, in using his or her vehicle for company purposes, assumes liability for his or her vehicle. All employees who desire to use their personal vehicles for company business must sign statements verifying that they have a current driver's license and vehicle liability insurance in at least the minimum amounts required by state law.

Mileage Reimbursement Alternate Policy 2 440.2

Employees of (COMPANY) who use their personal vehicle for company purposes will be provided an automobile allowance of (ADD DOLLAR AMOUNT) per month. This allowance is intended to compensate the employee for all costs related to the operation of his or her personal vehicle on company business. The employee assumes liability for his or her personal vehicle in work-related travel. Use of a personal vehicle is always for the employee's benefit and will never be required by the company Employees must sign a statement confirming that they have a valid driver's license and sufficient vehicle liability insurance.

Travel expenses between home and your work location are not reimbursable. Most company-related travel will originate from our company location. But in those cases where it is advantageous (time and distance considered) to leave directly from your place of residence, the request for reimbursement should be based upon total miles traveled for the company less normal daily mileage to and/or from your work location.

Mileage reimbursement will be approved by your supervisor/manager by submitting an expense report detailing the purpose of such travel, date of travel, and mileage traveled. All such expense reports must be submitted for approval as soon as possible but no later than (ADD DATE). Requests for reimbursement are due on the last working day of each month. The employee's reimbursement will be available on the third working day of the month following receipt by the vice president.

Travel Reimbursement 450

Comment: Travel is typically an important part of the cost of doing business because personal contact and communication are necessary to the success of many companies. The cost of travel and business conferences has become an increasingly substantial part of overhead especially for sales and service companies.

Employees should be required to make an advance travel plan by:

- contacting clients prior to the visit;
- coordinating visits to several proximate locations whenever possible;
- making definite itineraries; and
- confirming appointments in advance.

Naturally, a clear definition of the purpose of each business trip is essential. Travel reimbursement policies generally define the purpose of company travel and the business ethics to govern reimbursement. This policy should provide as much flexibility as possible so that an employee is not caught in any location without the flexibility to adjust his or her schedule to meet a particular situation.

Travel Reimbursement Alternate Policy 1 450.1

This policy establishes the general guidelines and procedures to be followed when business travel is required.

1. Travel-related expenses are to be detailed on the company travel reimbursement form.
2. Employees who prefer to use their personal vehicles for their convenience on company business, including trips to the airport, will be reimbursed at the standard company mileage rate, provided that the time and distance involved is reasonable under the circumstances.
3. All parking expenses and highway tolls incurred as a result of business travel will be reimbursed.
4. All air travel must be approved in advance by the vice president unless unavoidable. All travel will be by coach class whenever possible. First class may be used when coach class accommodations are not available or when traveling with a customer who is traveling first class. The duplicate airline ticket receipt should be attached to the company reimbursement form.
5. The company insures employees who fly when traveling on company business with a travel accident rider to our regular group insurance policy. Purchase of additional air travel insurance is not a reimbursable expense.

Note: *Delete this preceding statement if your company does not provide such travel insurance, but consider whether or not such insurance purchased by the employee should be reimbursable anyway.*

6. Employees should request advance approval for use of a rental car at their destination. If a rental car is used, additional insurance should not be purchased because of our

▶

Travel Reimbursement — continued Alternate Policy 1 450.1

existing insurance coverage. A copy of the rental car agreement form must accompany the travel reimbursement form.

7. Employees should select moderately-priced lodging convenient to their destination to minimize time and expense. A detailed receipt from the hotel or motel must accompany the reimbursement form unless such is unavailable, in which case, a credit card receipt is acceptable.
8. Employees must submit receipts for meals with the reimbursement form. Reasonable tips, when paid by the employee and noted on the receipt, will be reimbursed.
9. Travel reimbursement requests are due on the last working day of each month.

Travel Reimbursement Alternate Policy 2 450.2

All company travel, conference, and meeting expenses must clearly serve the objectives of the company and should not conflict with the ethical standards of our company. In preparing for company travel, prior approval must be obtained from the vice president by submitting a travel approval request memo detailing the itinerary, estimated cost, and business purpose of travel. If air travel is required, request the (VICE PRESIDENT) to make the reservations. All personnel will travel economy class unless extenuating circumstances require first class travel.

Lodging expenses are to be reimbursed at actual cost. Unless special circumstances dictate otherwise, mid-price lodging facilities shall be selected. Room accommodations will be honored only for one person per room, per night. Expenses for a nonemployee are not reimbursable. Exceptions include meals for a customer or business associate when discussing business or for other legitimate business-related meetings and conferences. Should a nonemployee companion accompany you on a business trip, the "single" rate for lodging should be noted on your copy of the bill and expense report.

Reimbursement for food and other incidental travel expenses are referred to as per diem expenses. Per diem is defined on the basis of the hours spent in travel, generally measured from point of departure to point of return. The full per diem allowance is (ADD DOLLAR AMOUNT) per day. Full per diem is granted for travel requiring an employee to be away from home for more than 15 hours; half per diem is granted for trips involving 6 to 15 hours and no per diem is allowed for trips less than 6 hours.

Note: *You may decide to reimburse employees for their actual meal and incidental expenses. Some companies give an employee the option to claim more than a modest per diem if they submit receipts showing expenses over the per diem.*

▶

Travel Reimbursement — continued Alternate Policy 2 450.2

Travel advances are intended to allow employees the convenience of using the company's money for business purposes while traveling. However, only reasonable travel advances will be granted and only on (ADD NUMBER) days' prior request. Typically, the travel advance will be equal to the per diem times the expected number of travel days unless the employee can justify a greater need. The advance must be accounted for on the travel reimbursement form by deducting it from the employee's claimed expenses.

All requests for reimbursement of company travel are due by the last working day of the month. Payment will be made to the employee by the fifth working day of the following month. If the travel advance exceeds the claimed expenses, employees shall attach a check to the expense report made payable to the company for the difference.

Footnotes

400 — Vacation

1. Cal. Lab. Code § 227.3.

Cross Reference Sheet

As your business grows, you may need additional policies to meet the changing needs of your business and employees. *A Company Policy and Personnel Workbook* ("CPPW" below) contains many additional policies which you may wish to consider. Plus, it offers companion computer software for IBM and Macintosh for those who want to speed up the process of typing and printing out policies.

This Cross Reference Sheet is designed to help you expand your policy manual to include policies found in CPPW. A "✓" indicates that substantially the same material is found in CPPW and *Developing Company Policies* ("DCP"). An "X" indicates that no such policy, chart, or form is found in CPPW or DCP. To find corresponding policies in DCP and CPPW, find the policy number under the column labeled "DCP". Immediately to the left of this policy number is the corresponding policy number in CPPW.

CPPW Policy Headings *(and DCP variations)*	CPPW	DCP
Foreword	✓	✓
Introduction	✓	✓
Develop and Maintain Your Policy Manual	✓	✓
Suggested Formats for Your Policy Manual	✓	✓
How to Use this Book	✓	✓
Final Thoughts Before You Begin	✓	✓
Chapter 1 Our Company	✓	✓
Welcome Letter from the President	1010	100
Company History *(and Philosophy)*	1020	110
Company Objectives	1030	X
Organization Chart	1040	X
Statement of Growth, Profit, and Business Plan	1050	X
Statement of Commitment to Employees	1060	X
Continuity of Policies — Right to Change or Discontinue	1070	120
Acknowledging Receipt of Policy Manual	1080	130
Chapter 2 Hiring Practices	✓	✓
Equal Opportunity	2010	200
Recruitment	2020	210
Employee Selection Process	2030	220
Sexual Harassment	2040	X

	CPPW	DCP
Medical Evaluations and Interviews	2050	×
Substance Abuse	2060	×
Smoking	2070	230
Employee Classifications	2080	240
Employee Safety	2090	×
Anniversary Date and Reinstatement	2100	250
New Hire, Rehire, Relatives, and Return to Work After Serious Injury or Illness	2110–40	260–80
Performance Improvement	2150	290
Terminations	2160	295
Chapter 3 Compensation	✓	✓
Equal Pay	3010	300
Position Descriptions	3020	310
Workday, Payday, and Pay Advances	3030–50	320–40
Overtime Compensation	3060	350
Meal and Rest Periods	3070	360
Flextime	3080	370
Performance Review and Salary Merit Increases	3090	380
Salary Administration	3100	×
Payroll Deductions	3110	390
Shift Premium	3120	×
Chapter 4 Employee Benefits *(and Expenses)*	✓	✓
Insurance	4010	×
Vacation	4020	400
Holidays	4030	410
Sick or Personal Leave	4040	420
Leave of Absence and Military Leave	4050	×
Medical Leave of Absence	4060	×
Bereavement Leave	4070	×
Jury Duty	4080	×
Voting	4090	×
Pension, Profit-Sharing, and Retirement Plans	4100	×

	CPPW	DCP
Chapter 5 Employee Expenses	✓	×
Employee-Incurred Expenses and Reimbursement	5010	430
Mileage Reimbursement	5020	440
Travel Reimbursement	5030	450
Use of Rental Car on Company Business	5040	×
Conferences and Meetings	5050	×
Professional Memberships	5060	×
Relocation of Current or New Employees	5070	×
Temporary Assignment Allowance	5080	×
Educational Assistance	5090	×
Required Management Approval	5100	×
Child Care	5110	×
Chapter 6 Miscellaneous Policies	✓	×
Announcement of New Positions	6010	×
Confidentiality of Company Information	6020	×
Employee Orientation	6030	×
Inventions and Patents	6040	×
Conflict of Interest	6050	×
Grievance Procedure	6060	×
Gratuities to Government Employees or Officials	6070	×
Gratuities to Customer or Supplier Representatives	6080	×
Political Activities	6090	×
Employee Privacy	6100	×
Telephone	6110	×
Dress Code	6120	×
Kitchen–Break Room	6130	×
Employee Recognition	6140	×
Visitors	6150	×
Recreational Activities–Sponsorships	6160	×
Outside Employment	6170	×
Employer Security	6180	×
Emergency Closings	6190	×
Parking	6200	×
Mail and Shipping	6210	×

	CPPW	DCP
Charts, Forms, and Outlines	✓	✓
Sample Policy	✓	✓
Sample Policy Manual Cover Page	✓	✓
Employee Orientation Checklist	×	✓
Organization Chart	✓	×
Employment Opportunity/Position Requisition	✓	✓
Interview Summary Sheet	✓	✓
I-9 Form	✓	✓
Employee Hiring Confirmation Form	×	✓
Employee Accident Report Form	✓	×
Exit Interview Guide	✓	✓
Position Description	✓	✓
Time Sheet	✓	✓
Payroll Advance Request	✓	✓
Overtime Approval Form	×	✓
Employee Work Plan and Performance Appraisal	✓	✓
Performance Appraisal	✓	✓
Performance Review Outline	✓	✓
Employee Performance Review	✓	×
Employee Work Update	✓	×
Company Evaluation Form	✓	×
Leave Request	×	✓
Grievance Form (Alternate Policy 2)	✓	×
Grievance Form (Alternate Policy 3)	✓	×
Authorization to Provide Information	✓	×
Consent to Release Information	✓	×
Cross Reference Sheet	×	✓

Business Formation and Planning

The Successful Business Plan: Secrets & Strategies
New Book available Summer 1991

Start-to-finish guide to creating a successful business plan. Includes tips from venture capitalists, bankers, and successful CEOs. Features worksheets for ease in planning and budgeting with the Abrams Method of Flow-Through Financials. Gives a sample business plan, plus specialized help for retailers, service companies, manufacturers, and in-house corporate plans. Also tells how to find and impress funding sources.

Starting and Operating a Business in... series
Book available for each state in the United States, plus District of Columbia

One-stop resource to current federal and state laws and regulations that affect businesses. Clear "human language" explanations of complex issues, plus samples of government forms, and lists of where to obtain additional help or information. This book helps seasoned business owners keep up with changing legislation. It also guides new entrepreneurs step-by-step to start the business and do what's necessary to stay up and running. Includes many checklists and worksheets to organize ideas, create action plans, and project financial scenarios.

Starting and Operating a Business: U.S. Edition
Set of eleven binders

The complete encyclopedia of how to do business in the U.S. Describes laws and regulations for each state, plus Washington, D.C., as well as the federal government. Gives overview of what is involved in starting and operating a business. Includes lists of sources of help, plus post cards for requesting materials from government and other agencies. This set is valuable for businesses with locations or marketing activities in several states, plus franchisors, attorneys, accountants, and other consultants.

Surviving and Prospering in a Business Partnership
Book

From evaluation of potential partners, through the drafting of agreements, to day-to-day management of working relationships, this book helps avoid classic partnership catastrophes. Discusses how to set up the partnership to reduce the financial and emotional consequences of unanticipated disputes, dishonesty, divorce, disability, or death of a partner.

Corporation Formation Package and Minute Book
Book and software for IBM-PC, available for Texas, Florida, or California

Provides forms required for incorporating and maintaining closely-held corporations, including: articles of incorporation; bylaws; stock certificates, stock transfer record sheets, bill of sale agreement; minutes form; plus many others. Addresses questions on regulations, timing, fees, notices, election of directors, and other critical factors.

Franchise Bible: A Comprehensive Guide
Book

Complete guide to franchising for prospective franchisees or for business owners considering franchising their business. Includes actual sample documents, such as a complete offering circular, plus worksheets for evaluating franchise companies, locations, and organizing information before seeing an attorney. This book is helpful for lawyers as well as their clients.

Develop Your Business Plan
Book

Comprehensive workbook guides the creation of a complete, professional business plan. Includes worksheets, flowcharts, assessment forms, income, and balance statements, plus illustrated examples to follow. (A selection of *The Executive Program® Book Club.*)

Software for IBM-PC & compatibles

StandAlone software with built-in word processing and spreadsheets save time in writing and formatting the text of a business plan and in calculating the required financial statements and projections. *Requires 512K of RAM plus hard disk, or dual floppy drive. No other software is required.*

How To Develop & Market Creative Business Ideas
Paperback Book

Step-by-step manual guides the inventor through all stages of new product development. Discusses patenting your invention, trademarks, copyrights, and how to construct your prototype. Gives information on financing, distribution, test marketing, and finding licensees. Plus, lists many useful sources for prototype resources, trade shows, funding, and more.

Business Formation and Planning (continued)

The Small Business Expert
Software for IBM-PC & compatibles

Generates comprehensive custom checklist of the state and federal laws and regulations any specific business must comply with. Allows comparison of doing business in each of the 50 states. Quickly responds to "what if" questions, such as, what are the comparative tax consequences of various actions, like taking out bonuses or setting up a trust? Built-in worksheets create outlines for personnel policies, marketing feasibility studies, and a business plan draft. *Requires 256K RAM and hard disk.*

Acquiring Outside Capital

The Loan Package
Book

Preparatory package for a business loan proposal. Worksheets help analyze cash needs and articulate business focus. Includes sample forms for balance sheets, income statements, projections, and budget reports. Screening sheets rank potential lenders to shorten the time involved in getting the loan.

Venture Capital Proposal Package
Book

Structures a proposal to secure venture capital. Checklists gather material for required sections: market analyses, income projections, financial statements, management team, strategic marketing plan, etc. Gives tips on understanding, finding, and screening potential investors.

Financial Templates
Software for IBM-PC & Macintosh

Software speeds business calculations including those in PSI's workbooks, *The Loan Package, Venture Capital Proposal Package, Negotiating the Purchase or Sale of a Business, Develop Your Business Plan, The Successful Business Plan: Secrests & Strategies.* Includes over 39 financial templates including various projections, statements, ratios, histories, amortizations, and cash flows. *Requires Lotus 1-2-3, Microsoft Excel, Supercalc 5, PSI's Spreadsheet (described in the Financial Management section of this resource list), or comparable spreadsheet and 512 RAM plus hard disk or two floppy drives.*

Develop Your Business Plan
Software for IBM-PC & compatibles and Macintosh

Software with built-in word processing and spreadsheets save time in writing and formatting the text of a business plan and in calculating the required financial statements and projections. *Requires 512K RAM plus hard disk or dual floppy drives. No other software is required.*

Managing Employees

A Company Policy and Personnel Workbook
Book

Saves costly consultant or staff hours in creating company personnel policies. Provides model policies on topics such as employee safety, leave of absence, flextime, smoking, substance abuse, sexual harassment, performance improvement, grievance procedure. For each subject, practical and legal ramifications are explained, then a choice of alternate policies presented.

Software for IBM-PC & compatibles and Macintosh

Software includes built-in word processing so no other software is needed. Policies are on disk so the company's name, specific information, and any desired changes or rewrites can be incorporated into the model policies before printing out a complete manual for distribution to employees. *Requires 512K RAM and hard disk and floppy drive, or dual floppy drive.*

Staffing A Small Business: Hiring, Compensating and Evaluating
Book

For the company that does not have a personnel specialist. Clarifies the processes of determining personnel needs; establishing job descriptions that satisfy legal requirements; and advertising for, selecting, and keeping good people. Over 40 worksheets help forecast staffing needs, define each job, recruit employees, and train staff.

Managing People: A Practical Guide
Book

Focuses on developing the art of working with people to maximize the productivity and satisfaction of both manager and employees. Discussions, exercises, and self-tests boost skills in communicating, delegating, motivating people, developing teams, goal-setting, adapting to change, and coping with stress.

Marketing & Public Relations

Marketing Your Products and Services Successfully
Book

Helps small businesses understand marketing concepts, then plan and follow through with the actions that will result in increased sales. Covers all aspects from identifying the target market, through market research, establishing pricing, creating a marketing plan, evaluating media alternatives, to launching a campaign. Discusses customer maintenance techniques and international marketing.

Publicity and Public Relations Guide for Businesses
Book

Overview of how to promote a business by using advertising, publicity, and public relations. Especially for business owners and managers who choose to have promotional activities carried out by in-house staff rather than outside specialists. Includes worksheets for a public relations plan, news releases, editorial article, and a communications schedule.

Cost-Effective Market Analysis
Book

Workbook explains how a small business can conduct its own market research. Shows how to set objectives, determine which techniques to use, create a schedule, and then monitor expenses. Encompasses primary research (trade shows, telephone interviews, mail surveys), plus secondary research (using available information in print).

EXECARDS®
Communication Tools

EXECARDS, the original business-to-business message cards, help build and maintain personal business relationships with customers and prospects. Distinctive in size and quality, EXECARDS get through even when other mail is tossed. An effective alternative to telephone tag. Time-saving, EXECARDS come in a variety of handsome styles and messages. Excellent for thanking clients, following up between orders, prospecting, and announcing new products, services, or special offers. *Please call for complete catalog.*

Customer Profile and Retrieval (CPR)
Software for IBM-PC & compatibles

Stores details of past activities plus future reminders on customers, clients, contacts, vendors, and employees, then gives instant access to that information when needed. "Tickler" fields keep reminders of dates for recontacts. "Type" fields categorize names for sorting as the user defines. "Other data" fields store information such as purchase and credit history, telephone call records, or interests.

Massive storage capabilities with 12 type fields and 8 tickler dates. Holds up to 255 lines of comments for each name, plus unlimited time and date stamped notes. Features perpetual calendar, scheduler, and automatic telephone dialing. Built-in word processing and mail merge creates form or individual letters, addressed to selected names. Prints mail labels, rotary file cards, and phone directories. *Requires 640K RAM and 80 column display. (Autodial feature requires modem.)*

How To Develop & Market Creative Business Ideas
Paperback Book

Step-by-step manual guides the inventor through all stages of new product development. Discusses patenting your invention, trademarks, copyrights, and how to construct your prototype. Gives information on financing, distribution, test marketing, and finding licensees. Plus, lists many useful sources for prototype resources, trade shows, funding, and more.

International Business

Export Now
Book

Prepares a business to enter the export market. Clearly explains the basics, then articulates specific requirements for export licensing, preparation of documents, payment methods, packaging, and shipping. Includes advice on evaluating foreign representatives, planning international marketing strategies, and discovering official U.S. policy for various countries and regions. Lists sources.

Mail Order

Mail Order Legal Manual
Book

For companies that use the mail to market their products or services, as well as for mail order businesses, this book clarifies complex regulations so penalties can be avoided. Gives state-by-state legal requirements, plus information on Federal Trade Commission guidelines and rules covering delivery dates, advertising, sales taxes, unfair trade practices, and consumer protection.

Related Resources from PSI Successful Business Library

Business Communications

Proposal Development: How to Respond and Win the Bid
Book

Orchestrates a successful proposal from preliminary planning to clinching the deal. Shows by explanation and example how to: determine what to include; create text, illustrations, tables, exhibits, and appendices; how to format (using either traditional methods or desktop publishing); meet the special requirements of government proposals; set up and follow a schedule.

Write Your Own Business Contracts
Book

Explains the "do's"and "don'ts" of contract writing so any person in business can do the preparatory work in drafting contracts before hiring an attorney for final review. Gives a working knowledge of the various types of business agreements, plus tips on how to prepare for the unexpected.

Complete Book of Business Forms
New Book available Fall 1991.

Over 200 reproducible forms for all types of business needs: personnel, employment, finance, production flow, operations, sales, marketing, order entry, and general administration. Time-saving, uniform, coordinated way to record and locate important business information.

EXECARDS®
Communication Tools

EXECARDS, business-to-business message cards, are an effective vehicle for maintaining personal contacts in this era of rushed, highly-technical communications. A card takes only seconds and a few cents to send, but can memorably tell customers, clients, prospects, or co-workers that their relationship is valued. Many styles and messages to choose from for thanking, acknowledging, inviting, reminding, prospecting, following up, etc. *Please call for complete catalog.*

PlanningTools™
Paper pads, 3-hole punched

Handsome PlanningTools help organize thoughts and record notes, actions, plans, and deadlines, so important information and responsibilities do not get lost or forgotten. Specific PlanningTools organize different needs, such as Calendar Notes, Progress/Activity Record, Project Plan/Record, Week's Priority Planner, Make-A-Month Calendar, and Milestone Chart. *Please call for catalog.*

Customer Profile & Retrieval (CPR)
Software for IBM-PC & compatibles

Easy computer database management program streamlines the process of communicating with clients, customers, vendors, contacts, and employees. While talking to your contact on the phone (or at any time), all records of past activities and conversations can be viewed instantly, and new notes can be added at that time. *Please see description under "Marketing & Public Relations" section on previous page.*

Business Relocation

Company Relocation Handbook: Making the Right Move
New Book available Fall, 1991

Comprehensive guide to moving a business. Begins with defining objectives for moving and evaluating whether relocating will actually solve more problems than it creates. Worksheets compare prospective locations, using rating scales for physical plant, equipment, personnel, and geographic considerations. Sets up a schedule for dealing with logistics.

Retirement Planning

Retirement & Estate Planning Handbook
Book

Do-it-yourself workbook for setting up a retirement plan that can easily be maintained and followed. Covers establishing net worth, retirement goals, budgets, and a plan for asset acquisition, preservation, and growth. Discusses realistic expectations for Social Security, Medicare, and health care alternatives. Features special sections for business owners.

Career Recordkeeping

Career Builder
Book

This workbook collects all of an individual's career-related data in one place for quick access. From educational details, through work history, health records, reference lists, correspondence awards, passports, etc., to personal insurance policies, real estate, securities and bank accounts, this manual keeps it all organized. Gives tips on successful resumés.

To order these tools, use the convenient order form at the back of this book or call us toll-free at: 800-228-2275

Financial Management

Financial Management Techniques for Small Business
Book

Clearly reveals the essential ingredients of sound financial management in detail. By monitoring trends in your financial activities, you will be able to uncover potential problems before they become crises. You'll understand why you can be making a profit and still not have the cash to meet expenses, and you'll learn the steps to change your business' cash behavior to get more return for your effort.

Risk Analysis: How to Reduce Insurance Costs
Book

Straightforward advice on shopping for insurance, understanding types of coverage, comparing proposals and premium rates. Worksheets help identify and weigh the risks a particular business is likely to face, then determine if any of those might be safely self-insured or eliminated. Request for proposal form helps businesses avoid over-paying for protection.

Debt Collection: Strategies for the Small Business
Book

Practical tips on how to turn receivables into cash. Worksheets and checklists help businesses establish credit policies, track accounts, and flag when it is necessary to bring in a collection agency, attorney, or go to court. This book advises how to deal with disputes, negotiate settlements, win in small claims court, and collect on judgments. Gives examples of telephone collection techniques and collection letters.

Negotiating the Purchase or Sale of a Business
Book

Prepares a business buyer or seller for negotiations that will achieve win-win results. Shows how to determine the real worth of a business, including intangible assets such as "goodwill." Over 36 checklists and worksheets on topics such as tax impact on buyers and sellers, escrow checklist, cash flow projections, evaluating potential buyers, financing options, and many others.

Financial Accounting Guide for Small Business
Book

Makes understanding the economics of business simple. Explains the basic accounting principles that relate to any business. Step-by-step instructions for generating accounting statements and interpreting them, spotting errors, and recognizing warning signs. Discusses how banks and other creditors view financial statements.

Controlling Your Company's Freight Costs
Book

Shows how to increase company profits by trimming freight costs. Provides tips for comparing alternative methods and shippers, then negotiating contracts to receive the most favorable discounts. Tells how to package shipments for safe transport. Discusses freight insurance and dealing with claims for loss or damage. Appendices include directory of U.S. ports, shipper's guide, and sample bill of lading.

Accounting Software Analysis
Book

Presents successful step-by-step procedure for choosing the most appropriate software to handle the accounting for a business. Evaluation forms and worksheets create a custom software "shopping list" to match against features of various products, so facts, not sales hype, can determine the right selection.

Financial Templates
Software for IBM-PC & Macintosh

Calculates and graphs many business "what-if" scenarios and financial reports. Over 39 financial templates such as income statements, cash flow, and balance sheet comparisons, break-even analyses, product contribution comparisons, market share, net present value, sales model, *pro formas*, loan payment projections, etc. *Requires 512K RAM hard disk or two floppy drives, plus Lotus or comparable spreadsheet such as our program called "Spreadsheet" listed below.*

Spreadsheet
Software for IBM-PC & compatibles

Full-featured spreadsheet comparable to Lotus 1-2-3, but far more economically priced. Includes an extensive statistical analysis package of over 30 built-in functions. Creates worksheets with up to 256 columns by 2048 rows, and displays graphs of the worksheet data. Has unique cell annotation feature for leaving notes explaining formulas or where certain numbers came from. Comes with detailed reference manual with tutorials for both beginners and experts. *Requires 384K RAM hard disk and one disk drive.*

To order these tools, use the convenient order form at the back of this book or call us toll-free at: 800-228-2275

PSI Successful Business Library / Tools for Business Success Order Form (Please fill out other side also)

BOOKS - Please check the edition (binder or paper) of your choice.

TITLE	BINDER	PAPERBACK	QUANTITY	COST
Accounting Software Analysis	☐ $ 39.95			
Career Builder	☐ $ 34.95	☐ $ 12.95		
A Company Policy and Personnel Workbook	☐ $ 49.95			
Company Relocation Handbook	☐ $ 49.95	☐ $ 19.95		
Complete Book of Business Forms	☐ $ 39.95	☐ $ 19.95		
Controlling Your Company's Freight Costs	☐ $ 39.95			
Corporation Formation Package and Minute Book CA ☐ TX ☐ FL ☐	☐ $ 39.95	☐ $ 24.95		
Cost-Effective Market Analysis	☐ $ 39.95			
Debt Collection: Strategies for the Small Business	☐ $ 39.95	☐ $ 17.95		
Develop Your Business Plan	☐ $ 39.95	☐ $ 17.95		
Export Now	☐ $ 39.95	☐ $ 19.95		
Financial Accounting Guide For Small Business	☐ $ 39.95			
Financial Management Techniques For Small Business	☐ $ 39.95	☐ $ 19.95		
Franchise Bible: A Comprehensive Guide	☐ $ 49.95	☐ $ 19.95		
How to Develop & Market Creative Business Ideas		☐ $ 14.95		
The Loan Package	☐ $ 39.95			
Mail Order Legal Manual	☐ $ 45.00			
Managing People: A Practical Guide	☐ $ 49.95	☐ $ 19.95		
Marketing Your Products and Services Successfully	☐ $ 39.95	☐ $ 18.95		
Negotiating the Purchase or Sale of a Business	☐ $ 39.95	☐ $ 18.95		
Proposal Development: How to Respond and Win the Bid (hardback book)	☐ $ 39.95			
Publicity & Public Relations Guide For Businesses	☐ $ 39.95			
Retirement & Estate Planning Handbook	☐ $ 49.95	☐ $ 19.95		
Risk Analysis: How To Reduce Insurance Costs	☐ $ 39.95	☐ $ 18.95		
Staffing A Small Business	☐ $ 39.95	☐ $ 19.95		
Starting and Operating A Business in... BOOK INCLUDES FEDERAL SECTION PLUS ONE STATE SECTION –	☐ $ 29.95	☐ $ 19.95		
SPECIFY STATES:				
STATE SECTION ONLY (BINDER NOT INCLUDED) – SPECIFY STATES:	☐ $ 5.95			
U.S. EDITION (FEDERAL SECTION – 50 STATES AND WASHINGTON, D.C. IN 11-BINDER SET)	☐ $295.00			
Successful Business Plan: Secrets & Strategies	☐ $ 39.95	☐ $ 19.95		
Surviving and Prospering in a Business Partnership	☐ $ 39.95	☐ $ 19.95		
Venture Capital Proposal Package	☐ $ 39.95			
Write Your Own Business Contracts	☐ $ 39.95	☐ $ 19.95		
BOOK TOTAL (Please enter on other side also for grand total)				$

SOFTWARE - Please check whether you use Macintosh or 5-1/4" or 3-1/2"Disk for IBM-PC & Compatibles

TITLE	5-1/4" IBM Disk	3-1/2" IBM Disk	MAC	PRICE	QUANTITY	COST
Company Policy & Personnel Software	☐	☐	☐	☐ $ 69.95		
★ **Company Policy Binderbook & Software**	☐	☐	☐	☐ $ 129.95		
Corporation Formation Package Software CA ☐ TX ☐ FL ☐	☐	☐		☐ $ 59.95		
★ **Corporation Formation Binderbook & Software** CA ☐ TX ☐ FL ☐	☐	☐		☐ $ 89.95		
Customer Profile & Retrieval: Professional	☐	☐		☐ $149.95		
Develop Your Business Plan StandAlone Software	☐	☐		☐ $ 69.95		
★ **Develop Your Business Plan Binderbook & Software**	☐	☐		☐ $ 99.95		
Financial Templates	☐	☐	☐	☐ $ 69.95		
The Small Business Expert	☐	☐		☐ $ 59.95		
Spreadsheet	☐	☐		☐ $ 99.95		
★ **Special Combination Software: Financial Templates & Spreadsheet**	☐	☐		☐ $129.95		
SOFTWARE TOTAL (Please enter on other side also for grand total)						$

Please add above totals on other side to complete your order.

PSI Successful Business Library / Tools for Business Success Order Form (see other side also)

Call, Mail or Fax to: PSI Research, 300 North Valley Drive, Grants Pass, OR 97526 USA
Order Phone USA (800) 228-2275 Inquiries and International Orders (503) 479-9464 FAX (503) 476-1479

Sold to: PLEASE GIVE STREET ADDRESS NOT P.O. BOX FOR SHIPPING

Name ______________________

Title ______________________

Company ______________________

Street Address ______________________

City/State/Zip ______________________

Daytime Telephone ______________________

Ship to: (if different) **PLEASE GIVE STREET ADDRESS NOT P.O. BOX FOR SHIPPING**

Name ______________________

Title ______________________

Company ______________________

Street Address ______________________

City/State/Zip ______________________

Daytime Telephone ______________________

Payment Information:

☐ Check enclosed payable to PSI Research (When you enclose a check, UPS ground shipping is free within the Continental U.S.A.)

Charge - ☐ VISA ☐ MASTERCARD ☐ AMEX ☐ DISCOVER Card Number: ______________________ Expires ____

Signature: ______________________ Name on card: ______________________

EXECARDS

ITEM	PRICE EACH	QUANTITY	COST
EXECARDS Thank You Assortment (12 assorted thank you cards)	$ 12.95		
EXECARDS Recognition Assortment (12 assorted appreciation cards)	$ 12.95		
EXECARDS Marketing Assortment (12 assorted marketing cards)	$ 12.95		
EXECARDS TOTAL (Please enter below also for grand total)			$

Many additional options available. Please request complete catalog.

PLANNING TOOLS

ITEM		NUMBER OF PADS
Calendar Note Pad	☐ **1991**	
	☐ **91/92**	
	☐ **1992**	
☐ **Progress/Activity**		
☐ **Make-A-Month**		
☐ **Milestone Chart**		
☐ **Project Plan/Record**		
☐ **Week's Priority Planner**		
Total number of pads		
Multiply by unit price:		x
PLANNING TOOLS TOTAL		$

UNIT PRICE FOR ANY COMBINATION OF PLANNING TOOLS

1-9 pads	$3.95 each
10-49 pads	$3.49 each
50 or more pads	$2.98 each

GRAND TOTAL

BOOK TOTAL (from other side)	$
SOFTWARE TOTAL (from other side)	$
EXECARDS TOTAL	$
PLANNING TOOLS TOTAL	$
TOTAL ORDER	$

Rush service is available. Please call us for details.

Please send:

_____**Successful Business Library Book Catalog**

_____**EXECARDS Catalog**

_____**PSI Software Information**

Use this form to register for advance notification of updates, new books and software releases, plus special customer discounts!

Please answer these questions to let us know how our products are working for you, and what we could do to serve you better.

Title of book or software purchased from us:_______________________________

It is a:
- ☐ Binder book
- ☐ Paperback book
- ☐ Book/software combination
- ☐ Software only

Rate this product's overall quality of information:
- ☐ Excellent
- ☐ Good
- ☐ Fair
- ☐ Poor

Rate the quality of printed materials:
- ☐ Excellent
- ☐ Good
- ☐ Fair
- ☐ Poor

Rate the format:
- ☐ Excellent
- ☐ Good
- ☐ Fair
- ☐ Poor

Did the product provide what you needed?
☐ Yes ☐ No

If not, what should be added?_______

____
____
____
____
____

This product is:
- ☐ Clear and easy to follow
- ☐ Too complicated
- ☐ Too elementary

Were the worksheets (if any) easy to use?
☐ Yes ☐ No ☐ N/A

Should we include:
- ☐ More worksheets
- ☐ Fewer worksheets
- ☐ No worksheets

How do you feel about the price?
- ☐ Lower than expected
- ☐ About right
- ☐ Too expensive

How many employees are in your company?
- ☐ Under 10 employees
- ☐ 10 – 50 employees
- ☐ 51 – 99 employees
- ☐ 100 – 250 employees
- ☐ Over 250 employees

How many people in the city your company is in?
- ☐ 50,000 – 100,000
- ☐ 100,000 – 500,000
- ☐ 500,000 – 1,000,000
- ☐ Over 1,000,000
- ☐ Rural (under 50,000)

What is your type of business?
- ☐ Retail
- ☐ Service
- ☐ Government
- ☐ Manufacturing
- ☐ Distributor
- ☐ Education

What types of products or services do you sell?

____
____
____
____

What is your position in the company?
(please check one)
- ☐ Owner
- ☐ Administration
- ☐ Sales/marketing
- ☐ Finance
- ☐ Human resources
- ☐ Production
- ☐ Operations
- ☐ Computer/MIS

How did you learn about this product?
- ☐ Recommended by a friend
- ☐ Used in a seminar or class
- ☐ Have used other PSI products
- ☐ Received a mailing
- ☐ Saw in bookstore
- ☐ Saw in library
- ☐ Saw review in:
- ☐ Newspaper
- ☐ Magazine
- ☐ TV/Radio

Where did you buy this product?
- ☐ Catalog
- ☐ Bookstore
- ☐ Office supply
- ☐ Consultant
- ☐ Other__________

Would you purchase other business tools from us?
☐ Yes ☐ No

If so, which products interest you?
- ☐ EXECARDS® Communication Tools
- ☐ Books for business
- ☐ Software

Would you recommend this product to a friend?
☐ Yes ☐ No

If you'd like us to send associates or friends a catalog, just list names and addresses on back.

Do you use a personal computer for business?
☐ Yes ☐ No

If yes, which?
- ☐ IBM/compatible
- ☐ Macintosh

Check all the ways you use computers:
- ☐ Word processing
- ☐ Accounting
- ☐ Spreadsheet
- ☐ Inventory
- ☐ Order processing
- ☐ Design/graphics
- ☐ General data base
- ☐ Customer information
- ☐ Scheduling

May we call you to follow up on your comments?
☐ Yes ☐ No

May we add your name to our mailing list?
☐ Yes ☐ No

If there is anything you think we should do to improve this product, please describe:_______________________

____
____
____

Thank you for your patience in answering the above questions. Just fill in your name and address here, fold (see back) and mail.

Name_______________________
Title_______________________
Company_______________________
Phone_______________________
Address_______________________
City/State/Zip_______________________

If you have friends or associates who might appreciate receiving our catalogs, please list here. Thanks!

Name______________________________

Title______________________________

Company______________________________

Phone______________________________

Address______________________________

City/State/Zip______________________________

Name______________________________

Title______________________________

Company______________________________

Phone______________________________

Address______________________________

City/State/Zip______________________________

FOLD HERE FIRST

NO POSTAGE NECESSARY IF MAILED IN THE UNITED STATES

BUSINESS REPLY MAIL

FIRST CLASS MAIL PERMIT NO. 002 MERLIN, OREGON

POSTAGE WILL BE PAID BY ADDRESSEE

PSI Research
PO BOX 1414
Merlin OR 97532-9900

FOLD HERE SECOND, THEN TAPE TOGETHER

Please cut along this vertical line, fold twice, tape together and mail. Thanks!